Sleeping with Monsters

Sleeping with Monsters
Readings and Reactions
in Science Fiction and Fantasy

by
Liz Bourke

Seattle

Aqueduct Press, PO Box 95787
Seattle, WA 98145-2787
www.aqueductpress.com

ISBN: 978-1-61976-123-0
Library of Congress Control Number: 2017937871
10 9 8 7 6 5 4 3 2 1

Cover: Lighthouse © Can Stock Photo / kirstypargeter

Cover and Book Design by Kathryn Wilham

Printed in the USA by Thomson Shore, Inc.

Acknowledgments

This collection wouldn't exist without Leah Bobet, who first prodded me into writing reviews for anyone other than myself. Abigail Nussbaum, the former reviews editor of *Strange Horizons*, and Bridget McGovern and the team at Tor.com, gave me other opportunities. I remain abidingly grateful for their support.

Over the years, a vast array of people have kept me alive, challenged me to be a better thinker and a better person, and generally been amazing to me. This litany begins with my mother, Lorna Bourke, and my late grandmother, Florence (1928-2013). Special mention goes to Jensen Byrne, Faith Nolan, Ross Edwards, Katie and John Schiepers, Christine Morris, Jane Carroll, Karl Kinsella, Conor Trainor, Cian O'Halloran, and Kate McNamara, who I didn't need the Internet to meet; and D. Franklin, Zoe Johnson, Foz Meadows, Amal El-Mohtar, Tansy Rayner Roberts, Sarah Trick, Chelsea Polk, Niall Harrison, Justin Landon, Stefan Raets, Sarah Wishnevsky, Amanda Downum, Fade Manley, Arkady Martine, Celia Marsh, Jodi Meadows, Fran Wilde, Jenny Thurman, Emmet O'Brien, Ginger Tansey, Aoife O'Riordan, Alis Rasmussen, and the many many others who first came into my life via a set of tubes.

Especial thanks must go, of course, to Aqueduct Press and to L. Timmel Duchamp and Kathryn Wilham, who in the course of producing this volume have had to put up with my scattershot approach to commas and semi-colons, and my love for both the sentence fragment and the run-on sentence.

Contents

Foreword

by Kate Elliott

Back in the Neolithic before the rise of the World Wide Web and the later explosion of social media, science fiction and fantasy review venues were few and far between. Seen from the perspective of an outsider, they were curated as objective stations where a few well-chosen and perspicacious reviewers might wisely or perhaps in a more curmudgeonly fashion guide the tastes and reading habits of the many. There is a kind of review style that parades itself as objective, seen through the understood-to-be-clear lens of earned authority, judging on the merits and never bogged down by subjectivity. Often (although not always) these reviews and review sites took (or implied) that stance: We are objective, whereas you are subjective. Even if not directly framed as objective, such reviews had an outsize authoritativeness simply because they stood atop a pedestal that few could climb. Controlling access to whose voice is seen as authoritative and objective is part of the way a narrow range of stories become defined as "universal" or "worthy" or "canon," when a few opinion-makers get to define for the many.

The rise of the world wide web and the explosion of social media changed all that. As voices formerly ignored or marginalized within the Halls of Authority created and found platforms from which to speak, to be heard, and to discuss, the boundaries of reviewing expanded. Anyone could weigh in, and often did, to the consternation of those who wished to keep the reins of reviewing in their more capable and superior hands. Influenced in part by the phrase "the personal is political," many of these new reviewers did not frame their views as rising atop a lofty

i

objective spire but rather wallowed in the lively mud of their subjectivity, examining how their own perspective shaped their view of any given narrative whether book, film and tv, or game.

It was in this context (in the webzine *Strange Horizons*, to be exact) that I discovered the reviews of Liz Bourke. Gosh, was she mouthy and opinionated!

I am sure Liz is never as blunt as she might be tempted to be; at times the reader can almost taste her restraint. Nevertheless, some of her reviews may make for uncomfortable reading. She jabs at issues of craft and spares no one from criticism of clumsy verbiage, awkward plotting, clichéd characterization, and lazy worldbuilding. She consistently raises questions about the sort of content in books that for a long time was invisible to many reviewers or considered not worth examining. Uncovering the complex morass of sexism, racism, classism, ableism, religious bigotry, and homo- and transphobia that often underlies many of our received assumptions about narrative is right in her wheelhouse. She says herself that this collection "represents one small slice of one single person's engagement with issues surrounding women in the science fiction and fantasy genre," and she uses this starting point to examine aspects embedded deep within the stories we tell, often aiming a light onto places long ignored, or framing text and visuals within a different perspective. In her twinned essays discussing how conservative, or liberal, epic and urban fantasy may respectively be, she both questions the claim that epic fantasy is always conservative while suggesting that urban fantasy may not be the hotbed of liberalism that some believe it to be: "popular fiction is seldom successful in revolutionary dialectic."

Strikingly, she is always careful to reveal her subjectivities up front by making it clear she has specific filters and lenses through which she reads and chooses to discuss speculative fiction and media. For example, she introduced her Tor.com *Sleeps With Monsters* column by stating up front her intention to "keep *women* front and center" as subjects for review in the column.

She writes (only somewhat tongue-in-cheek) that "Cranky young feminists (such as your not-so-humble correspondent) aren't renowned for our impartial objectivity." When she writes about the game *Dishonored*, noting its gender limitations, she concludes: "And if you do shove a society where gender-based discrimination is the norm in front of me in the name of entertainment, then I bloody well want more range: noblewomen scheming to control their children's fortunes, courtesans getting in and out of the trade, struggling merchants' widows on the edge of collapse and still getting by; more women-as-active-participants, less women-as-passive-sufferers. I would say this sort of thing annoys me, but really that's the wrong word: it both infuriates and wearies me at the same time. I'm tired of needing to be angry."

By refusing to claim objectivity, her reviews explode the idea that reviews can ever be written from a foundation of objectivity. People bring their assumptions, preferences, and prejudices into their reading, whether they recognize and admit it or not. The problem with reviews and criticism that claim or imply objectivity is that they leave no room for the situational but rather demand a sort of subservience to authority. They hammer down declarations. By acknowledging there are views that may not agree with hers, Liz creates a space where the readers of her reviews can situate their own position in relationship to hers, as when she enters into the debate over canon and declares that "canon is a construct, an illusion that is revealed as such upon close examination." She goes farther, as in her essay on queer female narrative, to specifically discuss the question within the frame of "the personal narrative and *me*" and how "the politics of representation" and the presence of queer women in stories changed her own view of herself.

As a reviewer Bourke talks to us as if we're in conversation. What a pleasure it is to read pithy reviews of often-overlooked work I already admire, as well as to discover books I need to read. She enthuses about writers whose work is "arrestingly unafraid of the tensions at its heart" as she writes about Mary Gentle's *The Black Opera*, and devotes a series of reviews to the groundbreaking 1980s fantasy works of the incomparable Barbara Hambly. She can be angry, as when discussing the use of tragic queer narratives in fiction as "a kick in the teeth," and express disappointment in writers who trot out the tired old argument that "historical norms may limit a writer's ability to include diverse characters." But there's also room for a lighter-hearted examination of, for example, C. J. Cherryh's *Foreigner* series in an essay that analyzes how the hero of the series, Bren Cameron, "rather reminds me of a Regency romance heroine—not for any romantic escapades, but for the tools with which he navigates his world." Her argument invites us to consider our own reading habits—the Regency romance as descended through Jane Austen and Georgette Heyer has become a sub-genre read and loved by many within the sff community—and thereby to see how cross-genre reading casts its influences.

This aspect of dialogue creates immediacy and intimacy as well as disagreement and even indignation. But think about what it means in the larger sense: situationally-oriented reviews create interaction. Just as every reader interacts with the text or media they are engaged in, so can reviews expand on that interaction. And if that makes Liz Bourke a rabble-rouser who pokes a stick into people's cherished assumptions and encourages us to examine and analyze and to talk with each other, then we are the more fortunate for it.

Introduction

What's in these pages?

This book comprises a selection of reviews and blog posts that first appeared at various locations on the Internet—*Strange Horizons*, Tor.com, and *Ideomancer.com*, as well as my personal blog, lizbourke.wordpress.com—between 2011 and 2015, along with previously unpublished review-essays. It doesn't contain *all* the reviews and blog posts I wrote for publication during that time, as that would make an unwieldy tome. And when I started to put this collection together, the question at the forefront of my mind was *what is its purpose?*

It turns out that's a less straightforward question than I expected it to be, in part because the component parts were originally written for different audiences and with different purposes in mind. The purpose of a review (which is a different thing entirely from the *point of criticism*, or the *point of writing about books*) is to communicate in a useful fashion the review-writer's subjective response to a text: to provide enough context that a reader can understand *why* the review-writer liked or disliked, loved or hated, or felt no strong feelings at all about the work at hand. The purpose of the blog posts I wrote for my *Sleeps With Monsters* column at Tor.com, on the other hand, is unequivocally hortatory: I was invited to contribute the column on the understanding that it would provide an explicitly feminist perspective, and I've used that platform to try to celebrate works or writers I think are under-recognized, to celebrate the achievements and the potential of women, and to try to critique antifeminist or sexist assumptions and tropes in narrative.

There are, naturally, similarities between my reviews and my blog posts. I'm a feminist: all my subjective responses to texts incorporate that perspective. *Sleeps With Monsters* is just a little louder, a little angrier, and more inclined to praise than critique—at least where books are concerned. A majority of the pieces in this collection come from *Sleeps With Monsters*, and ultimately, its purpose is more similar to *Sleeps With Monsters* than not: to be a little loud and angry. To celebrate the work of women in the science fiction and fantasy (SFF) field. To offer a snapshot, a limited glimpse, of what I think is best, most fun, most *interesting*.

Or what I thought at one point in time, at least.

I should note, however, that the choice of books to review and topics to include was guided by my own reading preferences. It's not an attempt to present a view of the field of *feminist science fiction and fantasy*; rather it represents one feminist's engagement with the SFF field, which is a wilder, woollier thing. Most of the works I talk about here matter to me in some way or another— or they *annoyed* me in a certain way. Snapshot of the reader as a young woman. Idiosyncrasy of the individual. But there's no such thing as an individual completely apart from society, either....

There are as many ways of writing about books, games, and visual media as there are readers, gamers, and viewers. I like to think of myself as a critic, as someone engaged in a conversation. That's the whole point of criticism, for me: taking part in conversation, opening it up, talking about *interesting things*.

But the project of criticism is always as much about the critic as about the text. Because I'm an imperfect feminist—especially when it comes to issues of intersectionality and representation— there are things to which I'm blind. There are great gaping gaps in my understanding of the world and of the history of women's writing; those gaps are reflected in what I read, what I watch, what I play, what I write about, what I choose to focus on. (The nature of the gaps changes over time, but their existence never will.) So there are gaps here, too.

I hope what's here is a useful contribution to the critical conversation. A springboard for discussion, a place to start—or to continue—talking about the role and reception of women's work in the SFF field.

Let's be honest. I'm not a theorist. I fell into writing about books (for money) as much by accident as by intent—the kind of accident that comes from looking for ways to turn limited skills and experience into coffee money. When I try for academic detachment, I feel like an impostor. I always have this feeling that all the people who spent their undergraduate years reading literary and feminist theory are laughing at me behind their hands. (I have academic training. As an *ancient historian*.) But one thing I do know: the issues described by Joanna Russ in *How to Suppress Women's Writing* (1984) with her characteristic cogency remain with us three decades on. *Strange Horizons*' "SF Count" has in recent years cataloged the way in which professional SFF review outlets tend to focus disproportionate amounts of attention on the work of men vs. that of women.

"At the level of high culture," as Russ wrote, "...active bigotry is probably fairly rare. *It is also hardly ever necessary,* since the social context is so far from neutral. To act in a way that is both sexist and racist, to maintain one's class privilege, it is only necessary to act in the customary ordinary usual, even polite manner" (Russ, 1984, 18).

Business as usual. Without constant, careful consciousness, its outcome is the continuing marginalization of voices from outside the assumed default. The canon of literary history in SFF is a construct. Whose voices are remembered—and whose forgotten—in public awareness is always part of a narrative about what is seen as important, and who, and why. I'm not trying to retell or preserve or recover the literary history of women in SFF, though I think that's really important: other, more knowledgeable people have done work like that far better than I ever could, such as Justine Larbalestier in her *The Battle of the Sexes in Science Fiction* (2002) or Helen Merrick in *The Secret*

Feminist Cabal: A Cultural History of Science Fiction Feminisms (2009). No: what I'm personally interested in, what moves me, is the literary present. The stories we're telling ourselves about who we are now and what we're capable of becoming.

By *we* I mean people outside the old assumed default. The (straight, white, cisgender, able-bodied) masculine default. It is still faintly radical to say *humanity* instead of *mankind*: if we can tell enough stories where humanity doesn't *have* a default setting, maybe one day all our voices will be held to be of equal value.

A body can hope. After all, what's the point of being young if you can't cling to idealism?

So what I've put together in these pages is a sort of wandering literary ramble: an excursion through some of the books that have grabbed my attention or piqued my interest or seemed in some way *good to talk about*. It's a personal little meander, filled with odd turns and bizarre choices, and contains more questions than answers.

My own journey along the highways and byways of SFF literature is still, I hope, only just beginning. I'm looking forward to finding new questions and developing *new* opinions, but for now—

Here Are Some Books I Read.

You'll Never Believe What Happened Next.

Part 1.
Moving Forwards, Looking Back

Discussions of books by Susan R. Matthews,
R.M. Meluch, Nicola Griffith, and Melissa Scott

An Exchange of Hostages
Sleeps With Monsters: Tor.com, October 16, 2012

Space opera. It's one of my favorite things. (Although, to be honest, I have a *lot* of favorite things.) Fast ships, shiny explosions, many technologically implausible things before breakfast... what's not to like?[1]

Recently—and by recently, I mean in the last couple of years—I've been made aware that there have been, and still are, more women writing in this subgenre than I'd previously suspected. Maybe I shouldn't be surprised, considering that my experience of reading space opera was for a long while largely shaped by what showed up in my local bookshop and on Baen's online backlist. Neither of which, with occasional honorable exceptions such as Anne McCaffrey, Elizabeth Moon, and C.J. Cherryh, put much in the way of female-authored militaristic space opera in front of me.

But there's a whole universe of women writing interesting space opera out there, and if, like me, you've managed to miss out, I want to introduce you to some of it.

Just one book to start with. A debut novel from 1997, Susan R. Matthews' *An Exchange of Hostages*.[2]

An Exchange of Hostages isn't the easiest book in the world to categorize: it's an intensely character-focused novel set on a

---

1 Rhetorical question. The amount of problematic assumptions, social and otherwise, repeated in space opera is plenty large. "How to be a fan of problematic things" applies (http://www.socialjusticeleague.net/2011/09/how-to-be-a-fan-of-problematic-things/).

2 For a good while, all of Matthews' books were shamefully out of print and hard to find. Fortunately, Baen Books acquired the rights to publish the Jurisdiction series as ebooks, and those books are now widely available electronically. This is good, because they deserve better than to be forgotten.

space station in a space operatic setting. I'm comfortable calling it space opera because succeeding books open the universe out into a broader canvas, but on its own it defies easy pigeonholing.

It's also a difficult book to love unreservedly. I confess that I do, but I have a soft spot for impossible situations, well-drawn characters, and people caught between the rock of duty and the hard place of personal integrity. And I admire it when an author succeeds in disturbing me by causing me to sympathize with—and to understand—characters who do terrible things as part of terrible systems, and never lets you forget that *none of this is right.*

Sherwood Smith called it an "unflinching look at the physical and emotional consequences of anguish." That's a pretty good description for Matthews' books: or most of them, at any rate.

Andrej Koscuisko is a surgeon. Much against his will, but in compliance with the wishes of his family, he has come to Fleet Orientation Station Medical to learn how to be a Fleet Chief Medical Officer under Jurisdiction, where he'll learn how to be a torturer and an executioner for the brutal and unforgiving system of government called the Bench. He finds his duty morally repugnant—he finds the whole system morally repugnant—but he also comes to discover that he has a terrible talent for the work itself and a capacity for taking pleasure in pain that repulses him on a moral level even as it attracts him on a physical one.

As a psychological exploration of the consequences of torture, it's markedly ambitious for a first novel. It extends beyond that, however, developing a thematic argument over the nature of freedom and constraint, a constant emotional tension strung between internal and external pressures. As a reader, you spend most of the book hoping Andrej will find some way out of the impossible set of choices permitted him—but *An Exchange of Hostages* refuses any easy way out. No matter what he chooses, Andrej can't stand outside the system. Whichever way he turns, he's complicit in causing harm.

The most he can do is try to mitigate the damage.

The internal conflict, the man of medicine constrained to commit atrocity, the man who hates himself for enjoying his work, is entirely compelling. Unshowily competent with sentence-level prose, Matthews shines when it comes to characterization, particularly in the relationship between Andrej and his personal security officer, the enslaved Joslire Curran. Matthews isn't shy about portraying the impossibility of any remotely fair association between the pair, although affection and loyalty develop between them anyway, mostly thanks to Andrej's unusual personal integrity.

(It takes, *An Exchange of Hostages* contends, unusual personal integrity to behave with any measure of decency when given—when required to exercise—absolute power over other thinking beings. It seems a logical argument, one born out by history.)

An Exchange of Hostages has its flaws. The third major character to have point of view here, Mergau Noycannir, another student at Fleet's inquisitor school, at times feels like an afterthought, only there to illuminate Andrej's good points by comparison with her failings. While the politics which she represents come to play a much larger role in subsequent volumes, her resentment of and competition with Andrej—and later, her determination to co-opt him for her patron—seems a touch on the predictable side. For a book otherwise so good at coloring matters in shades of grey, it's a little disappointing.

But not very. As I believe I mentioned above, I like it a lot.

A tight, focused, quiet novel, *An Exchange of Hostages* made the Phillip K. Dick nominations list for 1998. In its wake, Matthews was also twice a finalist for the John W. Campbell Best New Writer Award, in 1998 and 1999.

Nineteen ninety-eight's the year, of course, that saw the publication of Matthews' second novel, *Prisoner of Conscience.*

Is Atrocity Off-Limits or Fair Game?
Sleeps With Monsters: Tor.com, October 23, 2012

What are the rules for writing about atrocity? Are there any? Should there be? We come back and back and back around to the issue of rape, but what about torture, mass murder, genocide?

Susan R. Matthews has an unexpectedly compelling touch for atrocity. *Unflinching* is a word that I keep coming back to with regard to her books: science fiction and fantasy is rarely willing to look the human consequences of atrocity in the eye. Even less often does it find itself able to do so with nuance and complexity.

Matthews has a knack for working with horrific material in a way that acknowledges human capacity for humor, decency, affection, and survival without ever minimizing the horror. She also has a knack for writing stuff that really ought to come with nightmare warnings: *Prisoner of Conscience*, her second novel, is perhaps the book of hers which I appreciate most—but, O Gentle Readers, I'm not made of stern enough metal to come away unscathed from a novel that essentially deals with one long, drawn-out, stomach-turning war crime.

Or perhaps a series of them. It's a little hard to draw a clear distinction.

So, *Prisoner of Conscience*. It's a sequel to *An Exchange of Hostages*, and Chief Medical Officer Andrej Koscuisko, Ship's Inquisitor, is about to be reassigned from his relatively non-terrible position aboard the Bench warship *Scylla* to a penal facility at Port Rudistal. The Domitt Prison is home to hundreds of prisoners in the aftermath of an insurrection. And Andrej will be expected to exercise his inquisitorial function—to be a torturer—to the exclusion of all else, and to the detriment of his sanity.

Cruel and unjust as the rule of law is in Matthews' Bench universe, however, it has its limits. There are rules about who can torture and execute prisoners, and how that may be done. The Domitt Prison has been ignoring the rules from the beginning, to such an extent that genocide has been done. Andrej, distracted by the death of one of his security officers and by playing the torturer's role, is slow to realize that something is badly wrong. But for all his faults, Andrej is a man of honor. What he does for the rule of law is an abomination, but what's been going on at Port Rudistal is even worse. And it's up to him to put an end to it.

It's just as well there are a good few chapters of Andrej being compassionate and honorable and doctorly before we get to the prison, because reading *Prisoner of Conscience* is a kick in the throat and no mistake.

Not so much because of Andrej Koscuisko, although he's a strangely compelling bloke for a torturer. But because of two other characters through whose eyes we see: the imprisoned, doomed former warleader Robis Darmon, and Ailynn, a woman indentured to the Bench for thirty years, whose services the prison administration has purchased to see to Andrej Koscuisko's sexual comfort. Andrej may be, to an extent, at the mercy of the system, but he also has power within it. Darmon and Ailynn have none: in Ailynn's case, even her autonomy of thought is constrained by the device the Bench implants in those it condemns to servitude, the "governor."

Darmon suffers under Andrej's torture. Ailynn is not free to give or withhold consent. The horror of the Domitt Prison is impersonal: victims tortured, burned or buried alive, are not held up close to our view. Darmon and Ailynn are, and that puts the edge on the knife of empathy that Matthews keeps twisting all the way through.

It's a kick in the throat, but—unlike some other novels—I don't mind it much, because *Prisoner of Conscience* doesn't expect me to think any of this is okay. And I have rarely, if ever, seen similar material treated with half so much sensitivity.

Which is not to say the part where Andrej discovers that prisoners are going alive into the furnaces doesn't turn my stomach.

After *Prisoner of Conscience*, 1999's *Hour of Judgment* feels practically fluffy and hopeful by comparison. It's the first of Matthews' novels to draw back and show a bigger glimpse of the wider universe, politically and socially, beyond Andrej Koscuisko himself. It also probably has the least percentage of actual torture as any book to date, although with a depraved captain as his commanding officer, a secret warrant for his death, and his hope of getting away from being an Inquisitor thwarted, there's surely a lot of emotional strain on our old friend Andrej. A strain which is redoubled when his best-loved security officer, Robert Saint Clare, does something that the governor in his head should have prevented, and kills a ship's officer.

The lieutenant in question had it coming, by any stretch of the imagination. But if Saint Clare is found out, Andrej would be even more hard-pressed to protect his own. And Andrej Koscuisko has not damned himself for eight years for nothing.

Matthews' Jurisdiction novels are deeply focused on character and intensely interested in anguish, the dynamics of absolute power, and the tension between conflicting—I hesitate to say "moral," but perhaps "dutiful" will do—imperatives. I have yet to read science fiction by another author that takes these themes from a similar angle.

Angel of Destruction

Sleeps With Monsters: Tor.com, October 30, 2012

Because I've decided to indulge myself this week, I want to talk about one more of Susan R. Matthews' Jurisdiction universe novels, *Angel of Destruction* (2001). I'd hoped to be able to discuss Matthews' work in publication order, but since at the time of writing I'm still waiting for the second-hand copies of her non-Jurisdiction books, *Avalanche Soldier* (1999) and *Colony Fleet* (2000), to arrive, I'm just going to roll with what I've got today.

So, *Angel of Destruction.* Together with *The Devil and Deep Space* (2002), the next novel in the Jurisdiction sequence, it marks a significant change within Matthews' Jurisdiction universe. Previously, we've seen our protagonist, Andrej Koscuisko, act against the Bench only in—relatively—small ways, and only when in emotional *extremis. Angel of Destruction* and *The Devil and Deep Space* show characters acting against their unforgiving government in ways that are far more broadly subversive—and which have everything to do with prioritizing humaneness and justice over the rigid, inflexible, and *inhumane* rule of law and its application.

Angel of Destruction, while connected to the Koscuisko books, stands on its own and presents us with a new protagonist in the form of Bench Intelligence Specialist Garol Vogel, who had a bit-part to play in *Prisoner of Conscience* and a small but significant one in *Hour of Judgment. Angel of Destruction,* as far as I can tell from in-text clues, takes place a short time before *Judgment,* and probably explains why Garol Vogel is not in the best of humors during the events therein recounted.

Vogel, we learn, in the novel's very first pages, is responsible for negotiating the surrender of a fleet of commerce raiders—the Langsarik fleet, who fled to fight back when their home was annexed by the Bench. In exchange for fulfilling certain conditions, the Langsariks will be permitted to live and even perhaps eventually assimilate back into their home system. Vogel respects the Langsariks and particularly admires their leader, Fleet Captain Walton Agenis. He's determined to do the best for them that he possibly can, and the settlement at Port Charid, under the oversight of the Dolgorukij Combine, is the least terrible of their options.

But a year later, the region near Port Charid is disturbed by a series of raids. The raids leave little evidence, but all fingers point to the Langsariks. Walton Agenis swears to Vogel that her people can't have done it. He wants to believe her.

Matters are complicated by the presence of Cousin Stanoczk, a servant of the Malcontent—the peculiar religious order that seems to serve the Dolgorukij Combine both as its collecting-ground for cultural misfits and as its intelligence service—who takes an interest in a raid's single potential witness and the fact that in the aftermath of the Domitt Prison incident, the authorities are looking for a quick resolution to their public relations problem.

A quick resolution means blaming the Langsariks, if Vogel can't gather exonerating evidence in time. And as anyone who's been paying attention can guess…that means lots of dead Langsariks.

The structure of *Angel of Destruction* is part mystery, part thriller. The reader knows early on who's responsible for the raids—the "Angel" of the title refers to a very old and very secret terrorist organization within Dolgorukij society, one long thought wiped out—but the suspense comes from Vogel's need to put the pieces together and uncover the real culprits in time to save the Langsariks. (Or to figure out what to do, how to choose between his duty and his sense of justice, if it turns out he can't find the right evidence in time for it to do any good.)

There are a couple of things I really like here, apart from the fact that—shockingly!—all the murder and torture in this book is carried out by People Who Are Not Our Protagonists. Matthews is *very* good at writing character: she has a gift for evoking empathy. Here she's finally working with characters from a broad(er) palette of cultures, set at varying degrees of moral and/or physical hazard. It's also becoming clear that Matthews has a deft and subtle touch with political implications, when she gives herself room. (Has it been heretofore established that realistic and interesting politics in books are *some of my favorite things?* Then be thus advised.)

And, yes, I really like Walton Agenis. Walton Agenis is *interesting*.

Angel of Destruction is where we learn that life under Jurisdiction might be frequently terrible, but it's not *necessarily* unutterably horrible. It's a little bit more complicated than *An Exchange of Hostages* and *Prisoner of Conscience* implied: not much, perhaps, but a little.

Family loyalty, ethics against duty, secret conspiracies, politics, honor, characterization: *Angel of Destruction* hits so many of my narrative kinks it's not even funny.

Religious Revelation and Social Upheaval
Sleeps With Monsters: Tor.com, November 6, 2012

Today I want to talk about *Avalanche Soldier* and *Colony Fleet*, Susan R. Matthews' two standalone novels.

Avalanche Soldier isn't space opera. Instead, it's set on a planet that's turned its back on powered flight for religious reasons. Maybe it counts as planetary opera, but I want to mention it here because it's one of the few examples I've come across of science fiction with explicitly religious themes that also explores how religion and social unrest interact. It's not the most successful of novels on technical grounds: the pace is uneven, and the political background is insufficiently well-delineated to avoid confusion. But an interesting failure can prove far more entertaining than a novel that's technically successful but has no *heart*, and *Avalanche Soldier*, for all its flaws, has heart in abundance. Salli Rangarold, an avalanche soldier, abandons her post to follow first her AWOL brother, and then the new religious teacher he has found—a teacher who speaks to Salli's soul, whom Salli believes instantly is the prophesied Awakened One. But things are more complicated than that, and Salli has to grapple with a distrustful secular authority, riots, and her brother's newly discovered hard-line fanaticism, as well as her own religious conversion.

The content of religious conversion is something that science fiction seldom concerns itself with. All too often, the future is functionally atheistical or keeps its religions carefully compartmentalized, so it's always intriguing to see a different take on the matter, one that looks at conflicting experiences of the numinous and sets them against a background of social and political disturbances.

Colony Fleet isn't a species of space opera either. It's a story set around a generation-ship fleet about to arrive at the first of its destination planets. Tension exists between the castes that have arisen in the centuries since they set out: the Jneers monopolies the best food, the best resources, the cushy assignments, while the Mechs get more dangerous berths on the edges of the Fleet, jury-rigging equipment to cover shortages.

Hillbrane Harkover has been exiled from the Jneers, betrayed by one of her own, and sent on assignment to the Mechs. Initially disgusted to find herself among the lowest classes, Harkover comes to feel at home with them—learns to adjust, learns to appreciate the advantage that their adaptability and their distributed, communal methods of organization has over the Jneers' hierarchical and status-centered modes of doing business. When Harkover and the Jneer who arranged for her disgrace are assigned to the same mission, to perform forward reconnaissance on their destination planet in advance of the colony fleet's slower arrival—and when trouble arises due to the Jneer's over-confidence and selfishness—it's down to Harkover to put the good of the colony ahead of personal safety and figure out how to bring vital information back to the fleet.

In structure, *Colony Fleet* is something of a bildungsroman: quiet, character-focused, with an emphasis on social dynamics. Its flaws are less obvious than *Avalanche Soldier*'s, its pacing more assured, but there are moments when the background world-building seems oddly thin, as though Matthews hasn't thought through—or at least managed to communicate—the ramifications of her setup. For me this is a minor set of niggles and doesn't interfere with my enjoyment of the story, which is the kind of SF eucatastrophic adventure of which I would like to see more, but this isn't Matthews at the top of her game, either.

Or perhaps that's a judgment I'm making because neither *Avalanche Soldier* nor *Colony Fleet* grab me with the same kind of immediacy and intensity that the Andrej Kosciusko books do. Still, all things considered, they're good, interesting books, well worth a look.

Homosexual Torturers, Immortal Rulers, and FTL Fighter-craft: R.M. Meluch's *The Queen's Squadron*

Sleeps With Monsters: Tor.com, November 20, 2012

Sometimes I wonder how many science fiction novels feature torturers with homosexual tendencies. I have a feeling the final tally would disturb me.

No, don't tell me. I don't need to know.

R.M. Meluch's *The Queen's Squadron* (Roc, 1992) is among them. Fortunately, it's not a clichéd portrayal: *The Queen's Squadron* is an odd and, yes, ambitious, albeit in strange ways, wee book. I'm still not entirely sure what to think of it, although I *am* noticing something I can't call a trend, pattern is perhaps the better word, in Meluch's work, an undercurrent deeply influenced by the Classical world. Or at least delighted to salt in off-the-cuff references and throwaway names.

Take *The Queen's Squadron.* Some indeterminate time in the future, three nations share one world (not Earth, although Earth is mentioned) and skirmish in space: one, ruled by immortals who apparently *also* come from Earth, has something of an empire. One is neutral. And one is the nation of Telegonia, the "free mortals," who've been clashing on and off with the immortals' empire for quite some time. FTL space travel is only possible by means of "gates," with the exception of the c-ships of the Queen's Squadron, crewed by the elite fighter-pilots of the immortals' empire.

Immortals don't risk their lives. But one has. Maya of the Timberlines, formerly known as Ashata, chooses to join the Queen's Squadron under an assumed identity. Meanwhile, Telegonia has come up with a plan to cripple the immortals' empire for good. *Gotterdammerung.* War is coming. No, wait. It's already there.

The novel follows three strands. The story of Major Paul Strand, who knows the plan for Gotterdammerung and falls into enemy hands, surviving torture and Stockholm syndrome to return home. The story of Penetanguishene, last survivor of a race of people who know infallibly when someone is lying: first Paul's torturer, and afterwards a species of friend. And the story of Maya, as she learns to understand her comrades and comes to fall in unwilling love with the Squadron's commanding officer, Race Rachelson. As the story unfolds, and the war progresses towards the collapse of the immortals' empire, it becomes clear that the war—its outbreak, its progress, its conclusion—has been manipulated into existence.

Telegonia comes from the Greek Τηλεγόνεια, and means *born far away*. It's also the name of a lost epic from the ancient Greek world, about Telegonus, son of Odysseus and Circe. When Telegonus comes to Ithaca, he goes unrecognized and ends up killing Odysseus by mistake. I'm trying not to read too much into the connection of names in a novel that puts so much of its thematic freight in concealments—of information, of identities, of the person behind the curtain secretly pulling all the strings—but the coincidence, if indeed it is one, adds an interesting layer of resonance to a story whose themes are wrapped around the interplay of truth and power.

It does a couple of things that annoy me, particularly with regard to character, however. Meluch's characters in general seem to be facile constructions, rarely achieving any great depth. The ratio of female to male characters is skewed male, and it is notable to me that the one woman who has point of view and some personality ends up entangled in the orbit of the alpha male in her vicinity. It doesn't pass the Bechdel test in any meaningful fashion: not that all books have to, but here it seems like a missed opportunity.

It's an interesting book, with far more meat on its bones—far chewier—than Meluch's *Tour of the Merrimack* series books possess. It's not quite as *fun*, and I'm not entirely sure whether it's wholly successful in arguing its themes, but it's a solid, well-constructed space opera.

It's not half as problematic as the Tour of the Merrimack series either. This novel, I feel certain, doesn't deserve to be out of print.

R.M. Meluch's Tour of the Merrimack Series

Sleeps With Monsters: Tor.com, December 4, 2012

Today, we're continuing our focus on female writers of science fiction space opera (or at least, my interpretation of this category) with a look at the most recent works of R.M. Meluch: her Tour of the Merrimack series. Jo Walton has already discussed these books on Tor.com,[3] but I want to take another look at them from a slightly different perspective. (Because I'm contrary like that.)

Right, so. I like to play cheering section, and I find there's a lot to enjoy in R.M. Meluch's first four Tour of the Merrimack books. (I have yet, I confess, to read the fifth one.) I enjoy them bunches—but I also want to acknowledge the fact that there's a hell of a lot of problematic shit floating around here.

So this is not really going to be cheering-section time, I fear. The good points of Tour of the Merrimack are really a whole lot of fun. The setting has a Star Trek sort of vibe, complete with a Kirk-figure captain—but Star Trek in a nastier, much less forgiving universe. In Meluch's universe, both Earth and the reborn, star-spanning Roman Empire are threatened by an inimical alien race known as the Hive, which consumes everything in its path and is really hard to stop. There are swords on board spaceships, and good reasons for them to be there; there's spiffy space battle and tension and intrigue and caper and plot, fighter-pilots, enemies-turned-mistrusted-allies, and all the trappings of crunchy popcorn-fun space opera. Pulpy, is what it is: but pulp's not necessarily a bad thing.

Plus, it has an interesting alternate-universe twist.

3   http://www.tor.com/blogs/2012/08/romans-and-aliens-rm-meluchs-tour-of-the-merrimack-books.

I wanted, when I sat down to write about this series, to be able to be unmitigatedly enthusiastic: space opera! Romans! Fighter pilots! But I can't turn the critical part of my brain off—it would be irresponsible of me—so now that I've pointed out the really serious fun parts, I want to delineate some of its more problematic elements, most of which show up in the first book and remain in play throughout.

Politically Infuriating:

In the 25th century, it's *Rome IN SPACE* versus *USA USA!* These are the two great superpowers. The political and social culture of Space-Rome is characterized by strong inconsistencies: it is as much Hollywood Space Rome or Star Trek's Romulans as anything legitimately built from the philosophical, moral, and social influences of the Principate or the Dominate, and Meluch conveniently ignores the fact that the Roman Empire survived in the empire's Eastern half until the fall of Constantinople—the Byzantines called themselves *Romans*: that's why the Turkish name for the Balkan region was *Rumeli*. While, on the other hand, 2440's USA is never fleshed out but appears to possess a culture, a military superiority, and a sense of manifest destiny unchanged from the 20th century.

Meanwhile, the rest of the nations of Earth—a political block known as the "League of Earth Nations"—are characterized as supine and possibly treacherous fools who contribute little or nothing towards the war with the all-devouring Hive.[4]

This is mostly uncool by me, but it'd be much easier to shrug my way past these flaws (400 years sees a lot of cultural and

4   I'd like to footnote the fact that realizing how Meluch had chosen to characterize the representatives of non-USian nations of Earth in *The Myriad* physically made my stomach cramp with disgust. Why did I keep reading, you might ask? Because dismissing the rest of us is fairly well par for the course in US-produced space opera—so much so that it took me a re-read to properly register that Meluch took things a wee step further, and chose to throw in every Craven Over-Civilized Diplomatic Fool vs. Noble Military Hero stereotype she could get her hands on.

institutional drift, generally speaking—often gradual, but over that timescale, it should still be showing up as obviously present) were it not for the other major stumbling block to my happy enthusiasm presented in these novels.

Rape Culture, the Male Gaze, and Sadistic Homosexuals:

If anyone needs a primer on what rape culture is, go find one. Then you'll understand why it's wrong that there's a deeply disturbing line in *The Myriad* where one female character is described as unrapeable. Because she's so *easy*, you see, she doesn't know the word *no*.

There is also far, far too much male gaze roaming around here, and little-to-no counter-balancing female one. Every single on-screen female character is described in terms of their physical attractiveness (and in terms of their availability), and there are some rather ...*bwuh? It's the 25th century why is this still a thing?!* moments around the Merrimack's (stunningly beautiful) executive officer and how that beauty affects others' perceptions of her.

So much male gaze. I'm not joking, lads. It got annoying and tedious.

Said executive officer is one of the two more interesting characters, however. The other character who's more than a bare two-dimensional sketch is Augustus, a Roman "patterner," sharp-edged and sarcastic—who also happens to be the only gay character hereabouts, and who is also classified (by the reading the narrative keeps pushing, at least) as a sadist.

Does this begin to seem like a problem to you?

I agree with Jo Walton that if you can overlook or forgive the problematic shit—and there's a lot of problematic shit—they're entertaining novels that manage a really *interesting* trick with the twist in the end of *The Myriad* that informs and adds an extra layer to the narrative of succeeding books.

That's a choice you'll have to make yourselves, because when it comes to The Tour of the Merrimack, after I weigh up its good points and its bad ones…well, I find they come out about even.

"He Left," or How About That War, Then? R.M. Meluch's *Jerusalem Fire*

Sleeps With Monsters: Tor.com, December 11, 2012

Last time, I was a little unflattering about Meluch's most recent series, the Tour of the Merrimack. So I thought I'd leave my brief casting-of-the-eye over her work with a book I can be mostly heartfelt and enthusiastic about: 1985's *Jerusalem Fire*.

Jerusalem Fire. It's odd and imperfect, and some of its opinions, where it touches—briefly but emotively—on the Jewish and Arabic population of far-future Jerusalem, make me twitch. But as an examination of character, of the price exacted by war on two different men, it is an excellent novel and interesting science fiction.

I also think it falls under the heading of planetary opera, because it has some very interesting, culturally speaking, aliens. But I'm willing to be convinced otherwise.

The Na'id, a human empire, rule the stars, or most of them. A section of humanity who've decided that in order to eradicate bias based on race or religion, they will force everyone to assimilate to the Na'id creed and to interbreed in order to diffuse differences in phenotype. (Science says: I HAZ BIN MISINTERPRETED, but belief-systems have never actually *needed* to be amenable to logic in order to continue propagation. Moving on....)

This has worked out just about as peacefully as you'd expect.

The novel opens with Alihahd, whose nom de guerre means "He left," running from the Na'id. A pacifist, he opposes the Na'id by helping people flee from them. When his vessel is destroyed, he and his quasi-rescuer, Harrison Hall—whose cold curiosity, self-interest, and focus on revenge forms a foil to Alihahd's discomfort with responsibility and violence, and his passive desire to end his life—end up on the planet of Iry, where they become the guests of the Itiri warrior-priests, a race of aliens who have been no more than legend to most humans for thousands of years. But humans aren't legends to the Itiri, who've gone out into the wider universe in secret on occasion and brought home strays.

One of those strays is Jinni-Ben-Tare, a human youth become Itiri warrior-priest, who carries with him immense hatred of the Na'id, immense drive to survive, and a sublimated desire for revenge that finally finds expression when the Itiri, in the end, cast him out.

Both Hall and Jinni-Ben-Tare are, in a sense, Alihahd's mirror-images: Jinni-Ben-Tare more so, since, as we learn more about what made Alihahd the deeply damaged yet still imposing man he is, we learn that some of the same things shaped the human boy the warrior-priest used to be.

The "Jerusalem Fire" of the title refers to the city of Jerusalem on Earth, symbol of resistance to the Na'id. The city whose fall broke Alihahd, although not in precisely the ways one might expect. The city whose role as a symbol of the enduring nature of human perseverance and of the futility of killing other humans in order to end strife forms the central image of this novel. There are many ways to read that image—though I do think that it shows a certain lack of imagination to suggest that several thousand years on from the twentieth century no *other* creed will have joined Jews, Christians, and Muslims in claiming Jerusalem as a central site for their revelation—and it's certainly a powerful one.

For a science fiction novel, *Jerusalem Fire* is very low-key, quiet, and concerned with interiority, with the examination of character. Unusual in its quietude, it is, I think, also unusually successful *at* it, rarely ranging into the moralistic or the downright peculiar.

It does have flaws, of course. Its structure is odd, and its emotional conclusion uncertain, and I no longer find it normal to read a book with such a complete focus on the internal lives of its men and none at all on women. (Except in one extraordinarily squicky moment: I've reached the conclusion that Meluch is *immensely bad* at characterizing female sexuality.)

It is, however, worth one's time—and holds up surprisingly well for an SF novel that's older than I am.

Slow River by Nicola Griffith
Review: First appearance.

The Gollancz Masterworks edition of *Slow River* (2012, first published 1995) has an introduction by author Tricia Sullivan in which she describes Nicola Griffith's second novel as an "austere, meditative book." It's a very apt description here—as it would be for Griffith's later contemporary novels, *The Blue Place, Stay,* and *Always*—and not at all what I expected from a book that was described to me as cyberpunk. Perhaps it is in the tradition of cyberpunk, but it doesn't have the garish obsession with its own *cool shit*, or the in-your-face swagger I associate with that subgenre. No, *Slow River* is its own thing entirely: a quiet, striking, *powerful* exploration of growth, identity, selfhood, and self-actualization.

I often don't like the way that word is used, self-actualization, but it *fits* here in a way no other word does. For Lore, our main character, *Slow River* is a journey from powerlessness to confidence, from childhood to adulthood, from ignorance to knowledge and the willingness to *own* her own choices.

Lore is an heiress and a specialist in bio-remediation—her family's business is built on waste management and turning polluted water into fresh. Lore is also eighteen years old, the victim of a bungled kidnapping that leaves her naked, badly injured, and alone on a city street. No longer wealthy and powerful. No one.

A passing stranger—Spanner, con-artist and thief, grifter and predator, the woman who'll become for a time Lore's lover, protector, and exploiter—takes her home, tends her wounds, and takes Lore under her wing when Lore refuses utterly to return to the family that failed to pay her ransom. In Spanner's company, Lore learns to reinvent herself, learns to hide so that neither her family nor the police can find her—but the price of her new life is deception and crime, exploiting and being exploited, until Lore becomes someone she loathes. She leaves Spanner to become someone new: takes a dead woman's identity implant and a job at a waste management plant—the bottom rung of the workforce in a plant she'd be overqualified to run. Negotiating her new role with co-workers and supervisor and making friends is a new experience for Lore: one complicated by the need to work a last job with Spanner in exchange for Spanner's help in making Lore's ID stand up to inspection, and by the waste management plant's dangerously negligent cost-cutting measures, which Lore knows could end in disaster. In the end, Lore has to learn to reclaim herself: to face the betrayals of her family and move forward on her own terms.

Slow River is a layered narrative, structured around three strands across Lore's life to date. Lore in the present recounts her story in the first person: *Next time I dipped my hand into the river it would be as someone legitimate, reborn three years after arriving naked and nameless in the city.* The past Lore, though—the Lore of three years ago, bleeding and vulnerable in a strange city; and the child and adolescent Lore, alone even, perhaps especially, in the midst of her family—her narratives are told in third person perspective, estranging them from the *I* of the present: Lore as she is now is not the same person as she was before. These narrative strands interweave with and support each other, gradually—inevitably—building to the novel's culmination in their inter-related revelations and betrayals. *Slow River's* tension is interior and interpersonal, lying in its emotional beats more than in any physical peril: its sensibilities today read as literary as much as science-fictional ones.

Its science-fictional elements have aged well; twenty years on from its first publication, this still feels like a world that *could* exist: one that still reflects our own. Its matter-of-fact inclusion of sex and queer female sexuality may have been much more transgressive twenty years ago, but the centrality of queer women remains unusual in science fiction even today.

Like many of Griffith's novels, *Slow River* concerns itself with the consequences of violence and isolation, emotional as well as physical. In *Slow River* it is in the main the consequences of abuse—the secrets kept in Lore's billionaire family, the identity-stripping violence of Lore's kidnap, the exploitation and self-betrayal Lore falls into in Spanner's company—that predominate. Its real excellence for me, though, lies in how much, and how subtly, this is a story about healing, about remaking. Lore's job at the waste processing plant, turning contaminated water into the drinkable kind, mirrors thematically her growth as an individual within the novel's pages. Alchemical transmutation happens to people, too, *Slow River* seems to say—and you can never go back to who you were. Even if you want to.

A brilliant book, powerful and thought-provoking, and one that will stay with me for a very long time.

Trouble and Her Friends by Melissa Scott
Review: First appearance

The copy of *Trouble and Her Friends* that I own came into my hands quite recently, courtesy of an excellent second-hand vendor. It's a Tor hardcover from 1994, complete with its original jacket and original jacket blurbs from Gwyneth Jones and Joan D. Vinge and Roger Zelazny. It startles me: this is good book, interesting cyberpunk, and it's a novel I'd never even heard of until the 2010s—along with most of the rest of Melissa Scott's work.

I wonder if the reason I didn't hear of Melissa Scott's *Trouble and Her Friends* until it had been out of print for upwards of a decade is the same reason I didn't hear about Nicola Griffith's *Slow River* until it was published in the Gollancz Masterworks series? They both have female protagonists who are in sexual relationships with other women, and neither of them treats this as particularly remarkable: something to note, when such a portrayal is only just becoming ordinary, if still uncommon, in the science fiction and fantasy genre. I wonder, if these had been the examples of cyberpunk that were held up to me as the best the subgenre had to offer—instead of *Neuromancer*, which may be the type and model of cyberpunk but that I bounced off like a ping-pong ball—whether I would still have come away with the impression that cyberpunk was a landscape of juvenile male anarcho-nihilism? (I never said it was a *fair* impression.) I suspect not. I suspect I would have had a *much* more positive reaction to cyberpunk when I first came across it in my teens.

But I didn't. And for years I had no idea books like these existed. In recent years the dialogue in the science fiction and fantasy community has been about diversity and representation, with the inescapable conclusion that *things are getting better than they used to be*. Sometimes I wonder if this doesn't run the risk of crossing people who were writing books with quote-unquote "diverse protagonists" before it became a marketing point out of history. Well, no. I don't wonder. I know it does. How to stop this process of forgetting, when many examples went out of print soon after publication and can still be difficult to find? (Although at least *Trouble and Her Friends* is available as an ebook.) That's a question I don't know how to answer, except by taking long digressions like these.

So, *Trouble and Her Friends*. Why do I like it?

Nineteen ninety-four is twenty years ago and change, and yet the future of networked computing *Trouble and Her Friends* posits isn't all that terribly different to something we can imagine today. Less mobile, less versatile, and more geographically rooted—and occasionally looking a little much like Second Life—but, modulo the implants that permit the eponymous Trouble and her fellow hackers to interact with their version of the Internet as a full virtual reality environment, the *way* they make use of it feels familiar and reasonable in ways that a lot of cyberpunk doesn't—to me, at least.

Trouble and Her Friends opens after the US government has passed a new piece of legislation to outlaw the legally dubious things that hackers have been doing in cyberspace. Trouble and her lover and partner Cerise have been doing dubious things for years, but the new legislation means the consequences will be severe if they get caught. Cerise doesn't want to stop; Trouble does. The novel opens after Trouble has left both Cerise and her hacking career, and between the opening pages and the main body of the novel, some time—a couple of years—elapses.

When next we meet Cerise, she's working for corporate security—blackmailed into the job, having taken one to many chances with illegal work—and she has a problem. Someone is causing trouble for her company—among other companies—breaking and entering in the virtual world of the nets. Someone using Trouble's handle, and who her company's analyses thinks is likely to *be* Trouble. Her boss wants her to find them and shut them down—find Trouble, and involve the legal authorities. Cerise doesn't believe it *is* Trouble, but she's in a bind: her boss can bring more than ordinary pressure to bear on her. And she still resents Trouble for walking out on her.

Trouble, meanwhile, is living under her legal name of India, working—almost entirely aboveboard—for a small artistic commune of sorts. She has no idea anything out of the ordinary is going on, until an old friend from her hacking days shows up on her doorstep to warn her. In short order she finds herself questioned by the authorities, asked to leave the commune, and essentially on the run from the law. She takes the troublemaking of the new "Trouble" personally: it's an insult to her name, and she's determined to find them and make them stop—and reclaim her reputation.

Trouble and Cerise re-encounter each other, and decide (neither really trusting the other entirely) to co-operate in order to solve their mutual problem: sidestepping corporate security and national and international law enforcement in order to find the truth, triumph, and learn to trust each other again.

The climax is tense, the denouement satisfying: but the real joy of *Trouble and Her Friends* is the characters. Cerise and Trouble are very different women, but their separate personalities, their drive, their *voices*, come across very strongly. I would have happily read more novels about them—but, alas, that's not to be.

Definitely a book I recommend.

Part 2.
Future Imperfect

Discussions of books by Elizabeth Bear, Aliette de Bodard, Jacqueline Koyanagi, Stephanie Saulter, Karen Lord, Lauren Beukes, Kameron Hurley, Jaine Fenn, Ann Leckie, Nnedi Okorafor, and Carolyn Ives Gilman

Carnival by Elizabeth Bear

Review: First appearance

I returned to reread *Carnival* (2006), Elizabeth Bear's fifth novel and fourth science fiction outing, shortly after reading her *One-Eyed Jack* (2014) for the first time. *One-Eyed Jack* is likely to go down in literary history as one of Bear's quirkier, more minor works: a fantasy set in Las Vegas in 2002 that plays with layers of metafictionality and is engaged in dialogue not only with urban fantasy and the mythology of American cities and American histories, but also with the US and UK spy shows of the 1960s—in particular *The Man from U.N.C.L.E.*, *I Spy*, and *The Avengers*. Bear's engagement with the fictional spy partnerships of the 1960s is explicitly on display in *One-Eyed Jack*. Its visibility is a smack on the head: how did I miss the influence of *The Man from U.N.C.L.E.* and *I, Spy* on the central relationship in *Carnival* on my first half-dozen readings?

Answer: because I wasn't all that familiar with *The Man from U.N.C.L.E.* and *I, Spy* in 2006.

Vincent and Michelangelo once had a long career together as partners—and lovers—in Earth's intelligence services. But this future Earth isn't an egalitarian one, and it frowns on homosexuality. After a mission went catastrophically wrong, the true nature of their relationship was discovered. Vincent was allowed to retire, but Michelangelo was forced into re-education. All this is backstory—what's past is prelude, as the poet says—when the novel opens with them yoked back in harness for one final mission together, ostensibly a diplomatic embassy to arrange the repatriation of certain works of art, but in reality to sabotage their hosts. They were the only people that could be sent, because the planet New Amazonia is a matriarchy, which has reversed the gender hierarchy of Earth. Homosexual men are (barely) acceptable envoys for New Amazonia's culture, but heterosexual men are not. So Vincent and Michelangelo are back together—and neither of them know that the other plans to betray their supervisors and botch the assignment.

Meanwhile, all isn't exactly roses in the internal politics of New Amazonia. The locals are aware that Vincent and Michelangelo aren't merely diplomatic envoys, and local politics has generated its own set of plots and counterplots—not to mention a spot of homegrown terrorism from among those who believe that the men of New Amazonia shouldn't remain second-class citizens. Plots begin to coincide when Michelangelo is abducted, and it turns out that the teenage daughter of their host is involved.

Vincent, the man who can (almost) always tell when someone is telling him the truth or not, and Michelangelo, the man who can lie well enough to fool any lie-detector, form a complementary pair that mirrors the complementary duos of Illya Kuriakin (reserved and intense) and Napoleon Solo (sociable and charming) in *The Man from U.N.C.L.E.*, and Kelly Robinson (athlete) and Alexander Scott (Rhodes scholar) in *I Spy*. Bear complicates the homosocial intimacy and professional trust of the 1960s spy pairings with sexual intimacy and enforced (at least for a time) professional distrust. The arc of their narrative moves them from physical intimacy back toward both emotional and professional intimacy: their partnership is both tested and reintegrated on a stronger footing.

I could be projecting, mind you. *Carnival's* third protagonist is native New Amazonian Lesa Pretoria, who doesn't come as one half of a long-term spy pairing, and her narrative development is to my mind the most interesting among the three. She deals with betrayals, both professional and personal, and comes to look outside her society's norms and make choices to protect those she feels most bound to protect—her young son, for whom the roles New Amazonian culture allot to men would be a limiting trap.

Bear has said of *Carnival* that its literary forebears include "When It Changed" and *Farnham's Freehold*.[1] Their influences are visible, but thematically, it's more interested in problematizing our understanding of what makes for a "good" society. Earth and New Amazonia mirror each other in ways that become uncomfortably obvious after the reader's sympathies have been engaged on the part of New Amazonia: both cultures operate with fairly rigid gender roles, although on the face of it New Amazonia is more permissive in terms of accepted sexualities. But this interrogation of dystopias is carried out in the background to the spy-thriller of the main plot: it creeps up on you by stages, while you're paying attention to other things. (Shiny things, like alien remnants and fancy new technology and assassination attempts and explosions.) In many ways, *Carnival* really is a book of mirrors and masks, one that looks different depending on from which angle you approach it. It's arguing with many things, though it comes to few conclusions—and yet it makes its arguments quietly, as interested in telling a fun story with spies as it is with Making A Point.

And that makes it a very interesting book.

1   http://www.irosf.com/q/zine/article/10370.

Blown by the Winds of War—Aliette de Bodard's
On A Red Station, Drifting

Sleeps With Monsters: Tor.com, November 5, 2013

I don't know if it's possible to call Aliette de Bodard's *On a Red Station, Drifting* (from the UK's Immersion Press) a quiet work, although under other circumstances I might be tempted to do so.

Riven with tension so well-strung the prose practically vibrates under its influence, its contained setting and ever-tighter circling of consequences essentially subverts the popularly understood derogatory overtones of *domestic conflict*.

Linh, a magistrate, arrives at Prosper Station a refugee from a war that's tearing the outer edges of the Empire apart. Instead of staying with her tribunal—and dying with them, when the invading warlord's forces took the planet—she fled. Prosper Station is home to distant family, but Linh, educated, self-assured (verging on arrogant), an official used to power, is out of place on a station whose resources have been depleted by refugees, whose greater personages have all been called away by the exigencies of war.

Quyen is the most senior of the family left on Prosper Station. The lesser partner in a marriage alliance who expected to spend her life in domestic concerns, the position of Administrator of Prosper Station has fallen to her. And among her concerns as administrator is to find a place for Linh, to sort out theft and honor among the family, and to preserve the Mind that directs and controls the lived environment of the station: the AI that's an Honored Ancestress to the whole family. For the influx of refugees has put a strain on the Mind's resources, and things do not work quite as they should.

Quyen and Linh don't get along. Each sees in the other an unwarranted arrogance, a reaching-above their proper station; each resents the other for her attitudes and behaviors. This isn't helped by a large amount of pride on all sides, by Quyen keeping messages from Linh, and Linh keeping a dangerous secret: her memorandum to the Emperor on the conduct of the war may be taken as treason, and her presence on Prosper Station thus put all her relatives at risk of sentence of death.

This short novel—technically a novelette, but it feels as though there's meat enough for a novel here—is divided into three sections, each of which builds thematically on their own and in aggregate towards an emotional crescendo. The middle section has for its centerpiece a banquet welcoming an honored visitor to the station. The amount of tension, emotional and social, involved in the preparation of a meal—with poetry, calligraphy, everything right and proper—puts many an action sequence to shame.

You may have noticed I'm a little enthusiastic about *On A Red Station, Drifting*. If it has a flaw, it's that I would have dearly enjoyed more time, more background, more of the universe in which it takes place. It's not the too-frequent predictably American vision of the future, and I for one rejoice in its difference.

Although the conclusion feels a little rushed, it closes its emotional arcs out satisfyingly. *On A Red Station, Drifting* leaves the reader with a pleasant, thoughtful aftertaste. I recommend it highly.

While de Bodard has set other stories in the same continuity, there is as yet no full-length novel. I have to say, I hope she writes one there—or more than one.

A Rare Space Opera: *Ascension* by Jacqueline Koyanagi
Review: Tor.com, December 16, 2013

It's not every day you read a space opera novel featuring a queer woman of color who stows away on a starship. Still less often do you read a space opera novel that includes a main character who suffers from a chronic illness while not being *about* the illness, or one which includes respectful, negotiated polyamorous relationships.

A novel which embraces all these things? It might not be *unprecedented*, but it's pretty damn rare.

Ascension, Jacqueline Koyanagi's debut novel, is just that rare thing. Its diversity—its *perspective*—is not one we see very often, and that played a large part in how much I enjoyed it. Before I make any further comment, I want to state that right up front: I enjoyed this book a hell of a lot. (It's not *Ancillary Justice*, but not every debut can hit *that* high.) But my enjoyment aside, as a novel *Ascension* is structurally odd, makes some unusual choices, and has a number of first-novel flaws.

Alana Quick is a sky surgeon, an engineer barely making ends meet in the repair shop she runs with her aunt. But she dreams of space, and when a ship, the *Tangled Axon,* arrives looking for Alana's wealthy Spirit Guide sister Nova, she stows away in the hopes that they'll keep her on in a berth. The *Tangled Axon* needs Alana's sister in order to negotiate with Transluminal Solutions, the giant, powerful corporation from another dimension that has gradually been taking over the galactic neighborhood. Transluminal Solutions are the only people who might have a cure for the strange affliction that is slowly killing the *Axon*'s pilot. But Nova isn't interested in dealing with Transluminal Solutions at all, and instead of a simple job, Alana finds herself in the middle of desperate derring-do: first half a hostage, then a fugitive when the crew of the *Tangled Axon* are framed for genocide.

And that's before she starts falling in love with the *Axon*'s captain, who already has a lover. It's a situation fraught with a great deal of potential awkwardness, to say the least. An awkwardness not helped for Alana in the least by the fact that the *Axon*'s crew takes strangeness—like a pilot who fades in and out of view and an engineer who behaves like a wolf—for granted.

With its transdimensional commerce and spirit guides who directly manipulate the energies of the universe, *Ascension* bears a debt to the deep vein of fantasy that runs through science fiction. Its mode is space opera, light on the techsposition and heavy on atmosphere. On mature consideration, it owes as much or more to the influence of popular televisual science fiction as it does to the literary kind: we can see the echo of *Star Wars*'s Force and *Stargate*'s ascended beings, and perhaps especially *Firefly*'s misfit crew of down-on-their-luck semi-outlaws, struggling to get by in a frontier universe where establishment interests are always a hair's breadth from chewing them to pieces.

The effect of televisual influence is both structural and tonal. This makes for an odd reading experience, in terms of the peaks and troughs of the narrative's driving tension; the pacing of the emotional beats in particular seems more suited to the screen than the page. That's not a *bad* thing, necessarily, but it can be a little disconcerting, and make the narrative's progress feel a bit out of joint.

The novel's climax, on the other hand, is more than a *little* disconcerting. Doppelgangers, family drama, transdimensional travel, and the science-fictional equivalent of grand sorcery all come together, climax, resolution, and denouement within the same forty pages. It feels compressed to the point of confusion, as though Koyanagi ran out of either the space or the confidence to wrap up her story in anything less than a headlong rush. A little more signposting earlier in the narrative wouldn't have gone amiss: one doesn't really expect Evil Alternate Universe Doppelganger to only show up at the *very end* and be overcome within a handful of pages.

On the other hand, I might be biased, because I'm not that great a fan of doppelgangers in the first place.

Koyanagi has a knack for voice and character, even if her prose can at times verge on the rococo. For all its flaws, *Ascension* is a fun read for the most part, and one that has space among the stars for a wider variety of people than your average space opera. On the whole, I'm glad to see her debut in print, and I look forward with interest to watching her improve on it.

Gemsigns by Stephanie Saulter
Review: *Strange Horizons,* November 13, 2013

In the not-so-distant future, a medical catastrophe overwhelmed the world's population. The Syndrome caused massive depopulation and economic hardship: surviving it as a viable species meant genetically modifying almost every human being on the planet. But not all modifications are equal. The "norms" were modified only enough for survival and good health. But some humans were modified much more extensively: these genetically modified humans, "gems," were designed for specific tasks, to perform difficult and dangerous labor, while the rest of the human race recovered a stable and economically productive society. But the services provided by the gems were profitable for their creator companies even after the crisis passed. Seen as less than human, they lived in servitude.

All this is backstory, for *Gemsigns*—Stephanie Saulter's debut novel out of Jo Fletcher Books—opens on the cusp of change. After a century, political and social pressures have combined to free gems from servitude to the gemtech companies.

At least for now.

The novel opens just before the first major political conference to decide what rights the gems will be granted vis-à-vis the rest of the population. The gemtech companies want a return to the previous status quo, or as close to it as they can get. The gems want to be accorded the full rights of human beings. Caught in between is Dr. Eli Walker, genetic anthropologist, the man charged with providing this conference the answer to the question of *are gems really human*? Among other questions, such as: Are they especially dangerous? Can they be integrated into "norm" society?

Gemsigns wears its thematic influences on its sleeve. It is impossible to read this novel and not recognize in it the shadow of American black slavery and the ghettoization of the Jews in European history—not to mention the treatment of ethnic minorities by angry right-wing thugs. There is also a mythic undercurrent highlighted in the names of several important characters: Eli Walker shares a first name with the Eli of the Books of Samuel, whose name means Ascent. The leader of the gem community is called Aryel Morningstar; Aryel is a version of Ariel, *Lion of God*, and the cognomen Morningstar, in the Enochic apocrypha, refers to a fallen angel cast out of heaven for refusing to bow to Adam. (In the Christian tradition, of course, it refers to Lucifer.) The mythic overtones of Aryel's name are brought into high relief—and their deliberate nature confirmed—by the revelation of her abilities at the novel's climax.

Another character, a young child with an unprecedented ability, is called Gabriel: another angelic name, for an angel who commonly served as the messenger of Yahweh. Being named for a messenger is appropriate to Gabriel's ability. Although the social and political milieu of the novel is one in which religion is no longer a popular, mainstream phenomenon, its climax takes place on December 24th. At a symbolic level, Saulter appears to be combining the influence of the Exodus narrative with inspiration from the Christian Advent myth—but the allegory, for the most part, remains subliminal, which is an achievement in itself.

This is a novel that defies easy categorization. Near-future, it has the furniture of a modern dystopia—all-pervading surveillance, extremely powerful corporations, the lurking presence of the machinery of oppression—but it resists the tone and mood of dystopia. It is post-dystopian: in a sense, apocalypse recovery as opposed to apocalypse. Its focus on communities, on movements for change, on *hope* in all its difficulties and triumphs subverts dystopia's pervasive aura of gloom and despair.

Unlike many science fiction novels, *Gemsigns* is not a story of action and high-pitched confrontation. Personal violence and physical exertion form only a very small part of the narrative. Instead, it builds its tension in its quiet moments: when Eli Walker is conducting an interview with Aryel Morningstar; or when a reporter is unmasked in a gem community meeting and asked to leave, for example; or when several characters are discussing the prejudice-related assault on another gem; or when Gabriel's adoptive parents—both gems—and the gem community face the difficulties involved in keeping his abilities quiet to protect him.

Community is a word I keep circling back to, in relation to this novel. For while Saulter paints a strong picture, in Eli Walker, of a man caught between science, human ethics, and the pressures money and politics can bring to bear, it is the gem community that plays the novel's central role. Through several individual characters—most of them drawn in vivid colors—we see a range of responses to the situation with which they're faced, and the challenges of creating and maintaining a community of diverse individuals: a community under the shadow of prejudice that might yet be codified again into law. That Saulter, for the most part, maintains her narrative tension throughout is a testament to her skill and the brisk confidence of her straightforward prose.

Is it an entirely successful novel? No: *Gemsigns* employs a modified omniscient point of view, and Saulter walks a thin line in keeping from the reader things known to the characters. This kind of manipulation rings a false note when it's eventually revealed unless it's extremely well-done. Among the things Saulter keeps from the reader—along with every character other than Eli himself—are Eli's conclusions. My awareness of the contrived nature of this uncertainty made their eventual revelation fall a little flat. In addition, Saulter hits the symbolic notes that underscore her narrative a little too hard during *Gemsigns*'s climax and denouement, and blatancy takes away much of their power.

But this is a debut novel: one expects some flaws. And for a debut novel, it's both striking and accomplished. Although it's the first novel in a trilogy, *Gemsigns* stands complete in itself—but I'm looking forward to reading the sequel.

Karen Lord's *The Best of All Possible Worlds*
Review: *Ideomancer,* June 1, 2013

I've heard the term *domestic* SF used in relation to some works of the 1960s, often in reference to the stories of Zenna Henderson: a subgenre which takes the furniture of science fiction, but rejects the fantasies of political agency that often drive science fictional narratives, a subgenre within but at the same time tangential to the rest of the field.

The Best of All Possible Worlds is not a domestic work. It doesn't center around a domicile, around social interiors. But it is concerned with emotional interiority in a manner not often seen in the wider SF field, a novel immensely—one might even say *intensely*—personal in scope and concerned with small-scale actions, despite the world-destroying tragedy lurking in the story's near past and looming over its shoulder. This concern with the personal combines with a gentle nod at SF's mythic furniture to create a thematic, tonal continuity with Lord's first novel, *Redemption in Indigo*, although the two books are otherwise very different animals.

The Best of All Possible Worlds opens with the annual meditation retreat of a Sadiri man, Dllenahkh. His solitude is abruptly shattered when word comes—in the person of an old friend—to break the news: the Sadiri homeworld has been destroyed. All that remains of the Sadiri people are those who were off-planet when the attack came, and the Sadiri have gone from being the most influential people in the galaxy to a remnant who will need help to maintain their customs and their bloodline.

The narration picks up some time later with the first-person perspective of Grace Delarua, native and junior government official of Cygnus Beta, where a significant proportion of the surviving Sadiri men have come, searching for marriage partners among descendants of the long-ago Sadiri diaspora. Delarua and Dllenahkh work together on a cultural mission, traveling with a small team to Cygnus Beta's far-flung settlements, attempting to build the foundations by which the Sadiri will be able to intermarry with the taSadiri—descendants of diasporas. Their journey is a series of episodes through which Lord explores both her world in all its odd and fantastic variety, and Delarua and Dllenahkh's working—and eventually more than working—relationship. The influence of Vulcan on the Sadiri is visible, but the parallels are not exact, and this reader gradually came to realize that what on the surface seems a cheerful meandering straightforwardly personal little book is several times more complex than it first appears.

The Best of All Possible Worlds is an interesting novel on several levels. Its sensibility falls halfway between the SF novel and the fairytale. It uses SFnal images in a quasi-fairytale structure, whose mythic resonances operate on more universal levels than science fiction: Delarua and Dllenahkh visit people who do revenge-murder, an impregnable city with caste divisions, a secret monastery, the court of Faerie. And, too, the valencies of *The Best of All Possible Worlds'* metaphors are fluid. It has one foot in the river of science fiction and the other in the ocean of literary fiction: employing science fiction's concretization of metaphor in one instant and then in another literary fiction's metaphor as metaphor—labile, not concrete—maintaining a constant fluid tension between the two modes.

Although it's an utterly different sort of book, reading it, I found myself wanting to compare it to Angélica Gorodischer's *Trafalgar*. It enforces the same off-kilter alienation from the reading protocols of the SFF genre, a magic realist *mood* (though not as direct, or as obvious, as in *Trafalgar*) among the furniture of the scientific future.

It's not quite fish, not quite flesh, and not quite fowl, and perhaps it has an imperfect execution. But *The Best of All Possible Worlds* stretches the boundaries of the kind of stories it's possible for science fiction to tell. This is *one* reader who's very glad to have read it.

The Weight of Nested Paradoxes:
Lauren Beukes' *The Shining Girls*

Review: Tor.com, May 15, 2013

This is a novel about a time-traveling serial killer from the 1930s, his victims, the girl who survived him, and a burned-out, murder-beat journalist. It's competently, even *excellently*, written, makes brilliant use of a non-linear narrative to create and build tension, wears its American Literature influences proudly on its sleeve, and for me, despite its technical competence, *The Shining Girls* is ultimately a frustrating mess of a novel, one whose climax falls apart under the weight of nested paradoxes.

In 1931 Chicago, Harper Curtis kills a woman and takes a key from her pocket. The key leads him to The House, whose door opens on different times, where he is confronted by a room full of trophies from murders he will commit—because he has already committed them.

In 1991 Chicago, Kirby Mazrachi becomes an intern at the *Chicago Sun-Times*, working alongside Dan Velasquez. Two years ago she survived a horrific attack. Dan reported on it at the time. He's since moved into sports journalism, but Kirby is determined to use her time at the paper to track down the man who nearly murdered her.

Harper stalks his victims through time, taking and leaving trophies, watching them as children, killing them as adults. Kirby stalks newspaper cuttings and the families of murder victims, searching for any trace of her assailant, any evidence of his identity. The narrative slips back and forward in time, and both serial killer and survivor are driven, obsessive; both come across as essentially shallow characters. Hollow vessels. Mirrors in an empty room.

To be fair, I suppose I should be upfront with my biases. I've found sociopathy fundamentally boring for years, however horrific its results. Shorn of their inciting incidents, serial murderers, regardless of type, aren't actually all that interesting as *characters*. They aren't even particularly horrifying, any more than rabid animals are horrifying.[2] And Harper Curtis doesn't make a great deal of sense *as* a serial killer, although the magic-realism tone of The House sequences invites one to overlook the incomprehensible paradox of his victimology. (I'm pretty sure structuring your narrative inevitability around time paradox is a type of cheating....) And I've never really liked the tone of American Literature-with-a-capital-L.[3]

Among my problems with *The Shining Girls* are ones of a socio-political nature. Ana Grillo of The Book Smugglers has written about the gendered nature of its violence in her review.[4] Rather than recapitulate arguments over whether or not that violence is itself problematic, I want to point out that as far as I can tell, the non-white characters are all murder victims, with the exception of one black heroin addict whose POV is written in (to my non-specialist's reading ear) a subtly off rendition of African American Vernacular English.

In fact, I can pick at *The Shining Girls'* problems all day. It's the kind of book that goes down easy, but never seems to amount to more than the sum of its parts; well-written but ultimately hollow. I can't judge its success or failure because I can't figure out what kind of book it was trying to *be*, although I can see it was trying to be *something*. Is it all metaphor? What does it *mean*? Is there a thematic argument in here somewhere? I can't find it, and that's a sensation as frustrating as the wiggle of a loosened tooth.

2 Although possibly I've watched far too much serial-killer-thriller TV. After the fourth season of *Criminal Minds*, it's hard to find serial killers interesting in and of themselves anymore.

3 I know Beukes is South African, but the influences are obvious.

4 http://thebooksmugglers.com/2013/04/book-review-the-shining-girls-by-lauren-beukes.html.

Tonally, stylistically, it seems like the kind of book to appeal to readers of Niffenegger and Roth, a book to be welcomed in book clubs in which the likes of me never felt at home. But its structure rests on paradox: everything that will happen has already happened. In the end, the House is Harper is the House is Harper, and I'm still scratching my head over what just happened.

It's not so much a possession as an infection.
The House was always his.
Always him. (350)

In the end, while it's interesting in an abstract sort of way, *The Shining Girls* leaves me cold and rather unsatisfied. I'm going to be intrigued to see what other people make of it.

She'd Been Hoping for a Storm: Kameron Hurley's *Rapture*

Review: Tor.com, October 24, 2012

> Nyx sold her womb somewhere between Punjai and
> Faleen, on the edge of the desert.
> (Hurley, 2011, 1)

God's War, the first volume of Hurley's *Bel Dame Apocrypha* trilogy, opened with blood and violence and a kind of desperate amorality. So too does *Rapture* (2012), the trilogy's conclusion: but the blood and violence has aged with our protagonist, Nyxnissa so Dasheem, and matured. If *Infidel* (2011), the second volume, improved a dozen times on *God's War*, *Rapture* improves a good half-dozen on *Infidel*: this brutal, complex, morally grey novel is an unexpectedly brilliant capstone to one of the freshest approaches to science fiction I've read in recent years.

Includes Spoilers for *Rapture*:

The never-ending war between Nasheen and Chenja might be over at last, but Nasheen is on the brink of civil war, its political tensions exacerbated by the flood of unemployed and unemployable soldiers brought home by peace. A peace not everyone desires. Nyx, forced out of exile and retirement by the sisterhood of assassins she once belonged to, is compelled to track down a kidnapped politician. Alive, he's dangerous; dead, he could trigger a bloody coup and the resumption of war. There are aliens in the skies, and the scent of revolution on the ground—and not in Nasheen alone, for in Ras Tieg, Nyx's former associate Inaya has made herself the center of a shapeshifter rebellion.

With a ramshackle team of down-at-heel mercenaries, few with any cause to trust or follow her except for the money, and with a bel dame assassin and a mad magician for her guides, Nyx sets out across a perilous, flesh-eating desert towards the edge of the world to rescue a man she once left for dead. She knows she's being used. She doesn't know exactly how.

Hurley writes ferocious, uncompromising action, but she's also developing a very strong hand with character beats. *Rapture* is the culmination of arcs of growth that have been progressing since the early pages of *God's War*, incremental acts and decisions paying off in sometimes surprising ways. Bad decisions, too: there is an element, as Marissa Lingen noted, of "Let's get the band back together in order to kill them horribly."[5]

No, not everyone dies—but this isn't a book where everyone *lives*, either. Throughout this trilogy, Hurley appears to have been developing a thematic argument about the ethical possibilities open to people living in a world riven by violence, where long-term survival relies in large part on luck and selfishness. Or on being able to profit from someone else's violence. Even the landscape is inimical, filled with things that can kill inevitably, or unexpectedly: to disdain the violence that keeps you alive, or healthy, or wealthy, is to slide towards the hypocritical.

There are three things I really enjoyed about this book. The first is the way in which it pays off two volumes of build-up—including the aliens from the first book and the politics from the second. The way the nations we've seen in the first two books are beginning to change.

The second thing I love about this book—about the whole trilogy—is Hurley's organic take on future technology: *insects.* Bugs. Everything runs on insect power, and people eat them too. (These aren't books for those squeamish about arthropods.)

The third thing is character. Inaya, with her underground rebellion and backstabbing comrades and hard-fought, self-denying pitiless, ethics. Rhys, failed husband, a bit of a hypocrite, who wants nothing more than peace. Safiyah, a strange and ancient

5 http://mrissa.livejournal.com/833112.html.

magician. Nyx, capable of turning off her affections and going back to war.

> Nyx felt herself pulling away, boxing herself back
> up.... It was easy to become everything she hated
> again. Remarkably, maddeningly easy.
> (Hurley, *Rapture*, 11)

None of them are particularly likeable characters. All of them are, I find, compelling.

It would be unfair of me to rave about *Rapture* and fail to note that from another perspective, the whole trilogy is potentially problematic: the Bel Dame Apocrypha is set largely in societies that draw on Islamic influences, and particularly in *God's War* may be seen to condone the interpretation of an irreducible connection between Islam and violence. Having read the entire trilogy, I think otherwise:[6] but I suspect the combination of Islamic influences and brutality may result in problems for some readers.

As for me, I'm enormously pleased with *Rapture* and find it an excellent conclusion to an altogether satisfying trilogy. Kameron Hurley, I salute you—and look forward to seeing what you do next.

> Nyx gazed out toward the horizon, and weighed her
> options. There was a lot of thinking a person could do,
> in the long pause between what was, and what could
> be. She remembered the starship, bursting apart in the
> sky. She had done her part to usher in twenty years of
> peace. What Nasheen did with it was up to Nasheen.

> Now, she figured she'd either have a good tumble, or
> go down blazing. Either way, it was a fitting way to
> end things.

6 But my exposure to Islam is only that of an interested agnostic, it must be said.

The rain stopped. A pity. She'd been hoping for a storm.

"I'm retired," Nyx said—to the ocean, to the air, to Nasheen, to her visitor—and took her last drink. (Hurley, *Rapture*, 379)

Queen of Nowhere by Jaine Fenn
Review: *Strange Horizons*, April 26, 2013

I don't remember where I first heard, in relation to science fiction and fantasy, the axiom that the world of the novel's action is as much a character as the personalities in the narrative. World-as-character is the reason that "sensawunda" remains a term to conjure with in science fiction, and part of the reason, it seems, behind the journey/quest narratives in the fantasies of Jacqueline Carey, Elizabeth Bear, Steven Erikson, Robert Jordan, and others too numerous to name. In *Queen of Nowhere* (2013), Jaine Fenn opens a window on a fascinating and vivid science fictional world seen through the lens of an intriguing character—a world which, ultimately, proves more vivid and coherent than our protagonist.

Bez, a peripatetic hacker who moves from identity to identity as easily as shedding one set of clothes for another, is engaged in a private war against an enemy most of the rest of humanity believes defeated forever: the alien Sidhe, whose survivors look like human women but who have the power to manipulate and control minds. Bez, however, knows the truth: the Sidhe are still active and still working to manipulate the future of humanity's societies. And Bez, who became aware of their existence after one compelled her then-lover to commit suicide, doesn't believe they can be anything other than harmful to humanity. Her war is a war of information-gathering, of mining data and gathering evidence so that eventually, ultimately, she can expose all the Sidhe at work in human space—and neutralize their threat for good.

But Bez is hardly the only human with a hidden agenda. These others whom she discovers, and who discover her, may be both an aid to her and a danger—and I'm not certain the narrative entirely makes up its mind who's on whose side until very late in the game.

Queen of Nowhere is space opera, but a space opera informed by a post-cyberpunk aesthetic. Paul McAuley, in an interview quoted in David G. Hartwell and Kathryn Cramer's *The Space Opera Renaissance* (2006), advances a description of new space opera that may in part serve to illustrate Fenn's SFnal universe:

> New space opera—the good new space
> opera—cheerfully plunders the tropes and toys of
> the old school and secondary sources from Blish to
> Delany, refurbishes them with up-to-the-minute
> science, and deploys them in epic narratives where
> intimate, human-scale stories are at least as relevant
> as the widescreen baroque backgrounds on which
> they cast their shadows. There are neither empires nor
> rigid technocracies dominated by a single Big Idea in
> the new space opera; like cyberpunk, it's eclectic and
> pluralistic. (768-9)

Pluralistic is the word for *Queen of Nowhere*. No overarching authority governs humanity's settlements: each of the worlds, and the non-planetary "habs" which are Bez's native environment, operate independently, each with their own rules or standards. They are connected by freighters, information (in the form of faster-than-light communication, including the "beevee boards," an expensive interstellar version of Internet newsgroups), and for the sufficiently wealthy, starliners. The habs support a full spectrum of human life, from a poor underclass to the enormously wealthy, while interludes from the point of view of Bez's contacts (her agents and occasionally her pawns) provide a wider view of human space than Bez's (mission-oriented to the point of obsession) point of view can give.

Bez visits only one planet in the course of the narrative. The planet Gracen attracts tourists because its religion believes in "purifying congress"—sex. The planet's culture is sketched in outline: eschewing excess material wealth, it's a society which demarcates social space based on the gender of the participants. And on their partnership status: married women and single women socialize in different spaces to married and single men, a distinction which even extends to how virtual space—the "infoscape"—is constructed. Bez's interaction with this society—as an outsider, a person not interested in "purifying congress," someone trying to investigate an anomalous event without being revealed as inhabiting a false role—is one of the few times I've seen science fiction engage with and problematize tourism and the tourist-native encounter, as opposed to eroticizing the unfamiliar. Bez's problems as an outsider are the problems of someone who only has a visitor's understanding of the society, and only a visitor's access, but she's not particularly interested in its strangeness except inasmuch as it poses an obstacle to her endeavors.

It's also one of the few times I've seen sunlight cast as something strange and exotic: Bez, as a native of the space-based habs, has never been in direct, unfiltered sunlight before. And she's not entirely sure she likes it.

Queen of Nowhere is the fifth novel in a loosely connected series that began with *Principles of Angels* (2008). Although I'm told all five can stand alone, this is the first I've read, and it is possible that by starting here, one misses out on context that would provide *Queen of Nowhere* with additional emotional and/or thematic resonance, for on the whole the novel feels a little off-balance, particularly as we build towards the conclusion. The book begins well and vividly, with Bez being arrested by the local cops upon her debarkation from a starliner (under one of her many identities), and needing to rapidly and efficiently effect an escape. The action-oriented set pieces are among *Queen of Nowhere*'s highlights: the climax involves two assassins and a personal showdown with a Sidhe, with a solid clip and entertaining derring-do. In fact, when Bez is actively working towards completing a definite goal, the pace ticks along excellently. The story may lag slightly in the middle, but both beginning and conclusion whip things right along.

Characterization, though…. On her own, Bez is both fascinating and consistent. When she's interacting with other people, her characterization seems to waver. Take Imbarin Tierce, a man with power and an agenda that seems to tally with hers. Bez seems too ready to take him at his word, and not plan for the possibility of betrayal or manipulation, in ways which seem out of place with how the text tells us she behaves in relation to her mission. The denouement, too, feels to come from out of the blue, and—at least for me—changes the entire context of what has come before.

Though its flaws and oddnesses of characterization prove distracting at times, ultimately they don't take away from *Queen of Nowhere*'s vivid set-pieces and appealing worldbuilding. It's an energetic space opera, an interesting and entertaining entry in an old genre. On the whole, I found it an enjoyable novel: because of it, I'll be reading more of Fenn's work in the near future.

To Hell with Ideology: Elizabeth Bear's *Grail*
Review: Tor.com, February 28, 2011

Grail (2011) by Elizabeth Bear is the concluding volume of the Jacob's Ladder trilogy, after 2008's *Dust* and 2010's *Chill*.

It is perhaps a little awkward to review a book that mentions your name in its acknowledgments. So by way of disclaimer, I'd like to acknowledge that right here at the beginning. You can make your own judgments, I'm sure, on whether that constitutes a conflict of interest with regard to this review. And now that I've got that out of the way....

The generation ship *Jacob's Ladder* has survived internecine strife, tragedy, and conflict that almost destroyed the vessel. Now, fifty years on, with Perceval Conn secure in her position as Captain and the ship very nearly whole, they are approaching landfall.

Unfortunately, the planet of Fortune is already inhabited. Due to the length of their journey, the *Jacob's Ladder* has been leapfrogged in transit. The human inhabitants of Fortune are not entirely sanguine about the prospect of sharing space with the generation ship's crew. For during the centuries the *Jacob's Ladder* spent between the stars, the human race developed a means of reducing their conflicts—"right-minding," which eliminates dangerous "sophipathologies" such as fanaticism and religion. The unrightminded crew of the *Jacob's Ladder*, a ship with an New Evolutionist Bible in the corridor outside its bridge, present a disturbing prospect.

Neither is all the crew of the *Jacob's Ladder* entirely happy about making landfall. And with the re-emergence of two very old nemeses, Ariane Conn and the angel Jacob Dust, the situation aboard the ship spirals rapidly into open conflict.

Bear does a lot of things right with this book. "Sense of wonder" might be a cliché in science fiction, but the *Jacob's Ladder* has the weird and wonderful—and amazing—by the bucketload, from talking carnivorous plants to the necromancer's library of trees, and from winged engineers to the ship's angel Nova. The society of the planet Fortune, as seen through the eyes of its administrator, Danilaw Bakare, is briefly but believably drawn, and the clash of cultures that takes place when Danilaw meets the Jacobeans (I find myself wanting to type *Jacobites*, which is not exactly the same thing) rings both fascinating and true. This is the first time in three books that the *Jacob's Ladder* has been shown from an outside point of view, and Danilaw has a very refreshing perspective.

The characters about broke my heart several times over. This is not, I think, a book that is amenable to standing alone. The complicated and painful history of the Conn family is what provides the book's thematic arc with its emotional weight—which is not to say that someone who has no previous emotional invest-ment in the fate of the *Jacob's Ladder*, of Perceval, Tristan, Cynric, and Benedick Conn, Dorcas the Go-Back who wears the body of Tristan's long-dead daughter Sparrow, Mallory the necroman-cer, *et alia*, will not find the reading experience enjoyable, but I doubt they will find it quite as rewarding or satisfactory.

When one particular character bit the bullet, I will confess I cried. In the usual run of events, books do not make me cry.

True to form, the conclusion is tense, even nail-bitingly so. The final chapter (entitled "the feeble starlight itself": the chap-ter titles in all three books are not infrequently a joy to consider), in my opinion, doesn't quite leave enough space to assimilate the implications of the climax of events. Although the dangling emotional threads are, I suspect, left as tidy as one could in all conscience expect.

Grail is a damn good book, and one I truly enjoyed reading.

"Nothing quite clarifies your thoughts
like thinking you're about to die."
Ann Leckie's *Ancillary Justice*

Review: Tor.com, September 6, 2013

It's not every day a debut novel by an author you'd never heard of before derails your entire afternoon with its brilliance. But when my review copy of *Ancillary Justice* arrived, that's exactly what it did. In fact, it arrowed upward to reach a pretty high position on my list of *best space opera novels ever.*

Which is to say: *Ancillary Justice* (2013) is a novel about which I need to forcibly restrain myself from making high-pitched enthusiastic noises. YOU SHOULD ALL READ IT.

Ahem.

Ancillary Justice does many things extremely well. Told in the first person, it's a narrative in two parts: the present, which comprises a thriller plot (among other things) in which Breq, the last surviving ancillary soldier from the now-destroyed vessel *Justice of Toren* seeks to acquire a weapon with which Breq can kill the Lord of the Radch; and the past, where we learn what happened to set Breq on the path towards a quixotic and at first glance unattainable revenge. Leckie's prose is clear and muscular, with a strong forward impetus, like the best of thriller writing. It grabs you and urges you onwards. And her interleaved narrative is both clever and well-executed: clever, because alternating *past* and *present* heightens the novel's tension, ratcheting up the *what happens next?* factor, and well-executed because most of the breaks and pauses seem entirely natural, rather than forced.

It's a *good* thriller, even if some events come together in ways that appear too easily coincidental: Leckie writes a rousing climax and sticks the dismount.

And in the past sections, there's a really interesting exploration of the narrative possibilities of first person point of view for post-human characters: entities whose consciousness is distributed across multiple bodies. It opens up the field of view contained within the narrative *I*.[7] This post-human—but not post-fleshly—vision provides a significant part of the backdrop for *Ancillary Justice*'s events. Breq is an ancillary soldier, created from the dead bodies of conquered peoples, part of the distributed consciousness of the ship *Justice of Toren*. The Lord of the Radch, against whom Breq's revenge is directed, is not only multi-bodied, but also self-divided, parts of the Lord's consciousness carrying out secret actions against other parts.

As for worldbuilding: Leckie's really good at it. During the course of the story we spend time in three separate planetary or extra-planetary locations within and on the fringes of the empire known as the Radch. One is a planet recently conquered and not yet assimilated. One is not within the bounds of the empire. And one is a central hub, at the heart of Radchaai culture and dominion. Each are depicted not only with their own individual cultures and subcultures, but also with strong internal variations and divisions. Moreover, Leckie enlarges on an ongoing thematic critique of the nature and purposes of empires—particularly expansionist ones.

Up to now, I haven't mentioned the most striking aspect of *Ancillary Justice*.

The pronouns.

Radchaai language doesn't use gendered pronouns, usually. Since Breq is culturally Radchaai, *Ancillary Justice* uses only one pronoun to refer to all its characters, except where Breq is making an effort to be culturally sensitive. Leckie has chosen—in a move that can be contrasted with Ursula Le Guin's *The Left Hand of Darkness*—to use the English feminine pronoun throughout the text. It's an interesting choice, one that adds to the sense of

7   Apologies for the pun.

reading in a different culture, but also one which (as had to be pointed out to me) runs the risk of reinforcing our existing linguistic and cultural gender binaries.

On the whole, it's an ambitious trick and I think it works: every time Leckie uses a female-gendered pronoun to refer to a person whose gender has not been specified or has been specified as male it made me re-examine all my assumptions about how worlds and genders fit together. I am left to consider how gender is constructed and how I react to gendered and ungendered pronouns in text: trying to look at it from five different directions at once.

Half of them are *this is awesome*. Half of them are *why is this my first reaction?*

In sum, *Ancillary Justice* is both an immensely *fun* novel, and a conceptually ambitious one: it has many layers and many levels at which it can be enjoyed. And I can't hardly *wait* for the sequel.

Lagoon by Nnedi Okorafor

Review: First appearance

Lagoon (2014) is a remarkable novel. In some ways, it reminds me a great deal of Ian McDonald's *King of Morning, Queen of Day* (1991), although in their structures and narrative concerns the novels are entirely different. But both McDonald and Okorafor bring an intense sense of place, a local *specificity* to their respective novels: a rarity in a genre whose locales, when not invented wholesale, tend towards iterative versions of American cities, London (and more rarely Edinburgh), or Hollywood facsimiles of real places. The very specificity of *place* draws in and alienates the reader at the same time. An estrangement of the familiar. Set in Lagos, *Lagoon* combines the science-fictional, the mythic, and the quotidian to create a story of a city—the world—on the cusp of extraordinary change.

It's a hard book to get out of my head. It is doing so many things, and so many of them well, that I keep coming back to it: it's a good book, not just to think *about*, but to think *with*, too. For while I never connected on an emotional level with the three main characters—Adaora, marine biologist in a troubled marriage; Anthony, famous Ghanaian rapper; Agu, a soldier not at ease with violence who tried to defend a woman from his corporal—or with Ayodele, the extra-terrestrial woman who has come from the meteorite/spaceship that's crashed into Lagos' harbor, there is nonetheless something incredibly attractive about it; a multivocal playfulness, a *presence* and a subversive sense of humor that simultaneously combines and undermines ideas of genre and standard SFFnal categories of thought.

I keep coming back and back again to its sense of place. It is always startling to hit a novel using the toolbox of science fiction and set on Earth that doesn't take place in a sanitized or Americanized present or future. American SF is a wide field in itself, but I sometimes think that it can be limited by shared sensibilities and reading protocols, by the conversation with how things have been done before. This is changing slightly as ever more novels are produced, and as the Young Adult contribution to science fiction is taking a larger place in the conversation, but there is still a cultural *koine* there that elides a universe of experiences, a shared understanding built on the structure of American society and American mythology of *how things (should) work*. An understanding that doesn't always map on to other *koines*, other ways of thinking.

The American dominance of Anglophone literature may be unavoidable by numbers alone, but it does rather contribute to a sort of colonization of the imagination. *Lagoon* sets its face against this state of affairs, with its unapologetic focus on Lagos, on Nigeria and Nigerian characters—and the odd Ghanaian. Okorafor is in an interesting position as an author; as the American-born child of Igbo Nigerian parents, as a professor of English at a major university, as a writer of genre fiction—it would be easy, it would be *facile*, to see in her life the combining and subverting of ideas, of categorization, that is also present in *Lagoon*. Whether this is true or merely a projection is in any case moot: it's the work that concerns me here, and it strikes me that *Lagoon* occupies a sort of conceptual crossroads in speculative fiction, a playfully liminal transgressing of categoric boundaries.

The first "eroticizing" "transgression" (permit me a small amount of irony) lies in setting an alien-invasion/first-contact narrative *not* in Washington DC or London, Sydney or New York, those bastions of imperial power, but in Lagos. It is sometimes pointed out that many of the tropes of science fiction, particularly the alien invasion narrative, are taken from the histories of colonialism: they envisage an Other doing to an "us" constructed as US American or British (and usually a white, masculine us) something very similar to what the colonial powers did (and do) during their imperialist *floruit*.[8] But *Lagoon* sets its first-contact narrative within multiply colonized Lagos, and with its invasion inverts the usual paradigm, the usual *structures*, of the alien invasion story wholesale.

There are other crossings of categories within the story: religious, social, linguistic—for significant amounts of dialogue are rendered in Nigerian Pidgin, alongside the standard English(es) of the rest of the text—and even of species. But perhaps the most playful categoric transgression is the way in which *Lagoon* joins the science-fictional scenery of the first-contact story to an atmosphere of the mythic, to a magic-realist incorporation of spirits and gods. That kind of semantic mingling isn't quite the done thing in speculative fiction! But for *Lagoon*, it works, and works well.

It's a really interesting alien invasion story. It has *layers* of things going on.

---

8 See also John Rieder, *Colonialism and the Emergence of Science Fiction* (2008).

"Which self should she aspire to know?"
Carolyn Ives Gilman's *Dark Orbit*

Review: Tor.com, July 15, 2015

I can't say I've ever heard a bad thing about any of Carolyn Ives Gilman's work. *Dark Orbit* (2015) is the first of her novels that I've read, and it certainly lives up to its reputation. And to the promise of its first opening lines:

> In the course of Saraswati Callicot's vagabond career, she had been disassembled and brought back to life so many times, the idea of self-knowledge had become a bit of a joke. The question was, *which* self should she aspire to know?

Dark Orbit is a striking work of science fiction, and knowledge—self-knowledge, and how the knowledge of *other* people can shape a person—is at its heart. It is sharp and glittering and rather more interested in the philosophy of its physics than it is in the science. It's also a novel about First Contact and the limits of science's ability to classify data that cannot be *seen*. And damn, is it one *hell* of a novel.

Saraswati Callicot—Sara—is an exoethnologist and an independent spirit. Returning from a long stretch in the field with nothing to show for her work, one of her patrons recruits her to ride herd on a scientific mission to a newly discovered and utterly *peculiar* potentially habitable planet. Her real job is to keep an eye on a possibly unstable crewmate, her patron's relative. Thora Lassiter was a member of the interplanetary elite and a diplomat, until her prophetic delusions contributed to a revolt on the planet Orem. Her presence on this scientific mission is intended to keep her out of sight and out of mind, lest she provoke even further unrest. Sara is supposed to make sure she's safe and not going embarrassingly bonkers.

The scientific mission arrives to find a crystalline planet, laced with dark matter, which provides odd readings for their sensors. When a crewmember dies aboard ship—their head cut off, neither murderer nor murder weapon to be found—the scientists of the mission find their work restricted by the head of the security team. Then, on a trip to the planet, Thora mysteriously disappears.

The scientific mission believed the planet to be uninhabited. But they were wrong. It's home to a community of the blind, who have a very specific vocabulary for navigating their world, and who rely on perceptions that the sighted cannot grasp. And Thora finds herself among them, in passages under the planet's surface. As Sara, aboard ship, strives to understand the nature of the planet and to manage the botched First Contact with its peoples—while navigating murky political waters and worrying about the presence of a murderer—Thora, on the planet below, confronts her own past and perceptions in darkness. In order to return to her crewmates, she has to learn to use the same perceptions—quasi-mystical ways of perceiving and knowing—that the planet's inhabitants have mastered. If she can't, both the scientific mission and the native inhabitants are likely to perish in the face of a danger that neither, separately, will be able to avoid.

Dark Orbit is told largely from Sara's point of view, with long sections recounted as excerpts from Thora's "audio diary." They're both fascinating and compelling characters, but the nature of this technique encourages the reader to see Sara's narrative as reliable, and to consider Thora in the light of an unreliable narrator: we are told from the beginning, after all, that she has in the past been subject to delusions. But as the story progresses the reader comes to see both Sara and Thora as equally reliable—or unreliable—narrators, and is forced in the process to confront assumptions about the validity of different kinds of perception and different perceptual outcomes. That the scientific mission itself is divided into departments with different theoretical approaches to knowledge, and that the native inhabitants have different approaches and outcomes as regards perceiving and knowing than the scientists of the mission, returns us again to the theme of knowledge.

Dark Orbit is a peculiar novel, by turns sharp and gentle, cynical and idealistic, empiricist and mystical. But its characters are strongly drawn, its universe is richly sketched, and its prose is sheer delight. It is deeply compelling in its peculiarities and probably one of the best novels of science fiction that I've read in the last few years. And it's *fascinating*.

Part 3.
The Fantasy of Political Agency

Discussions of books by Stina Leicht, Molly Tanzer, Nicole Kornher-Stace, Seth Dickinson, P.C. Hodgell, Martha Wells, Kate Elliott, Violette Malan, Barbara Hambly, Kari Sperring, Sherwood Smith, Amanda Downum, Katherine Addison, Mary Gentle, Marie Brennan, Elizabeth Bear, and Beth Bernobich

Approachable Epic Fantasy: *Cold Iron* by Stina Leicht
Review: Tor.com, July 17, 2015

Cold Iron (2015) is Stina Leicht's third novel. With it, Leicht moves away from urban fantasy and toward epic in the new gunpowder fantasy mode. *Cold Iron* is the opening volley in The Malorum Gates series—and to judge from the amount of ground this novel covers, it's a series that's going to do a *lot* of epic in a relatively short space of time.

It is also a rather better, and strikingly less boring, book than its opening pages portend.

Cold Iron opens with Nels, a kainen crown prince—the kainen are a race of people taller than the human norm, all possessed of varying degrees of magical powers, including the ability to magically force other people to do their will, simply by instructing them to—who initially comes across as self-absorbed, spoiled, whiny, and ineffectual. Nels' only distinguishing factor is his lack of the command magic that is especially characteristic of the royal family of Eledore. But fortunately—for the reader, if not for Nels—tragedy strikes! Disbarred from the succession and forced into the army due to Eledorean taboos on the shedding of blood, Nels becomes approximately fifty times more interesting, and so does the novel. There are more point-of-view characters: Nels' twin sister Suvi, whose naval ambitions have been interrupted while she takes up the role of crown princess, and Nels' friend and lover, the apprentice healer-sorceress Ilta. With this cast, *Cold Iron* rapidly builds up towards *very entertaining indeed*.

Flawed—of which more later—but very entertaining.

Nels, Suvi, and Ilta are faced with an intransigent array of problems: an invasion by the resolutely unmagical but technologically more adept humans of Acrasia; a smallpox epidemic made worse when magic goes wrong; and the machinations of

Nels and Suvi's paternal uncle Sakari, who seems determined to take the reins of power into his own hands—at no small cost to Nels, Suvi, and Eledore itself. As Nels struggles with the responsibilities of military life, including hostile senior officers, enemy action, insufficient supplies, and men who don't trust him, Suvi must navigate court life and a mission at sea to acquire an alliance with the Waterborne nations, while Ilta is put under house arrest when her attempt to inoculate herself against smallpox gives rise to a magically more potent strain.

The war with Acrasia is going badly, and Nels' commanding officer is a sociopath. Meanwhile, among the Waterborne, Suvi has to deal with assassination attempts, a magical duel, and battles at sea. And in the background lurks an ancient danger, against which—it appears—only the Eledorean royal family can stand. As the Acrasian forces close in around Eledore's plague-wracked capital, Nels, Suvi, and Ilta are reunited in their nation's darkest hour. If they cannot avoid their uncle's betrayal and stand against the Acrasians, they'll just have to save what they can.

In *Cold Iron*, Leicht has written an approachable, entertaining epic fantasy, peopled with engaging characters and replete with dramatic incidents. I confess that lately I've been having a spot of argument with epic fantasy: most of the time I want it to be either *less boring* or less full of deeply unlikeable people. Fortunately, despite its length, *Cold Iron* avoids the worst perils of droning epic fantasy, and its characters, despite our initial introduction to Nels, are anything but unlikeable.

But *Cold Iron* has its flaws. Leicht has a tendency to skip large chunks of time between chapters and to signal these cuts only sketchily, with little summary of anything that has taken place in the intervening weeks or months. This is a little annoying. Also on the annoying side is my feeling that Leicht has got sea battles and life at sea *all wrong*—but it's been some time since I've sailed on a tallship, or even sailed at all, so one should not take my word for it.

Cold Iron might not be the very best example of epic fantasy around: I'm not inclined to rave about its prose or polish, and it *is* working with some familiar tropes—plus gunpowder. It remains to be seen whether or not the next volume is going to break new ground. But *Cold Iron* is plenty entertaining, and it's good enough that I'm definitely looking forward to finding out where the story goes next.

Vermillion by Molly Tanzer
Review: lizbourke.wordpress.com, July 11, 2015

Molly Tanzer is an award-nominated author of short fiction. With several collections already to her name, *Vermillion* (2015) is her debut novel, and it's a peculiar book.

Not peculiar *bad*, mind you. Just peculiar. There's enough material and sheer badass bizarre worldbuilding in Vermillion to do for any three other novels, and Tanzer sticks in all of it in a single volume. It makes for an odd, off-balance experience, in terms of immersion and structure. And yet it works, somehow: Tanzer has sufficient command of the tools of her craft to make the novel work as a unity.

But I get ahead of myself. *Publishers Weekly* described *Vermillion* as a mix of "steampunk and ghost story," but that's rather misleading. *Vermillion* reminds me rather more of a modern-day penny dreadful or dime novel, chock full of incidents and events—but with far better characterization than is typical of either.

Nineteen-year-old Lou Merriweather is a psychopomp. The daughter of an English father and a Chinese mother, she's inherited her father's business in 19th century San Francisco, and she's making a decent living sending ghosts, shades, and geung si (a sort of Chinese undead) on to the afterworld, whether or not they want to go—while passing for a man. That is, until she hears that young men from Chinatown who went away in search of work have gone missing somewhere in Colorado. And until one of them comes home dead in a crate full of patent medicine called "the Elixir of Life," and well on the way to becoming a geung si. Lou doesn't especially want to investigate what's happened to them, as her skills are more suiting to placating spirits than tracking down the living, but there's no one else willing and able to go. And with a conspiracy apparently disappearing young Chinese men, her conscience—not to mention her mother—doesn't leave her much choice.

Her quest into Colorado leads her to a ruthless but friendly young man called Shai and a sanatorium known as the Fountain of Youth. The Fountain of Youth is run by a doctor who's also a vampire—and Shai's lover—and who's just a touch on the megalomaniac side. Not only is Dr. Panacea running the sanatorium to bring him a semi-constant supply of human "food," but he's been keeping the Chinese workers prisoner to help build him a flying machine. Lou finds herself in the middle of a pretty sticky situation, and she's not just risking her own life. Because by coincidence the sanatorium is playing host to her childhood friend Bo Wang, who's dying of consumption, and with whom she's been in love for a very long time—even though he himself loves another man. And another of the sanatorium's patients, teenaged girl Coriander—who's been dispatched to the Fountain of Youth by her parents in the hope that the doctor can cure her of her patently unnatural attraction to other women—involves herself in Lou's investigations.

And everything blows up in their faces. The desperate action of the climax almost belongs in a different book entirely, as allies and enemies square off in open fighting while Dr. Panacea launches his man-made dragon into the sky. Can Lou successfully save herself and friends old and new? And what happens, afterwards?

Vermillion is a hell of a ride. Action interspersed with introspection; conflict with scenery; otherness with belonging. It has talking sea lions and tribes of sentient bears whose treaties with the United States forbid the building of railways; it has monster-hunters and psychopomps. And it is interested in outsiders, people caught between communities or pushed outside of them. (It doesn't shy away from depicting anti-Chinese racism, for example, but it's just as happy to show friendly relationships that cross race, class, and gender lines: it's not, for example, a particularly heteronormative book.)

Lou is a fascinating character, whose youth and whose position as the child of immigrants determines how she interacts with the world. Her brashness, combined with her innocence, makes her point of view both interesting and believable. And while *Vermillion* is unevenly paced, it's still remarkably compelling. I enjoyed reading it.

And I'm really rather looking forward to seeing what Tanzer does next.

Falling In Love with Nicole Kornher-Stace's
Archivist Wasp

Sleeps With Monsters: Tor.com, July 28, 2015

This book. This *book*. In the past few years, there've been a handful of books I count it a privilege to have read—a handful of books with which I fell instantly and deeply in love. It's a short list: Ann Leckie's *Ancillary Justice* (2013) and *Ancillary Sword* (2014); Katherine Addison's *The Goblin Emperor* (2014); Elizabeth Bear's *Karen Memory* (2015). I might spot you one or two others, depending on the day, but these are the ones that hit me right on an emotional level, where pleasure in the quality of writing combines with a straight shot to my narrative hindbrain: *this is our stuff! This is OUR THING!*

Nicole Kornher-Stace's *Archivist Wasp* (2015) has added itself to that list. I didn't expect it to: at a brief glance, it sounded a little too peculiar. But then I came across Amal El-Mohtar and Ana Grilo (of *The Booksmugglers*) discussing its merits on Twitter—and when people like that recommend a thing, I try to take notice.

Wasp is the Archivist. Her job is simple: hunt ghosts in a world that teems with them, long after a technological apocalypse. And, if she can, find out from them about the apocalypse that broke the world. But ghosts don't speak.

As Archivist, Wasp is an outcast, marked from birth by the goddess Catchkeep to do her work. Or so Catchkeep's priest has always said, at least. In order to become Archivist, Wasp killed the Archivist before her. And every year, she has to fight—and kill—to keep her role, against three other girls marked as she is. (*Archivist Wasp* opens with the latest of these fights and its immediate aftermath, and Kornher-Stace's skill and command of voice is immediately apparent.)

Wasp's life is solitary and brutal, and looks set to be short. At least, until she encounters a ghost that does speak. A ghost who offers her a bargain that might help her escape. A ghost who wants her help. Accepting his bargain will take her on a journey to the underworld in search of the ghost of the partner he thinks he betrayed. Maybe Wasp will make it back. Maybe she won't. Soon she becomes invested in the search for the ghost of Catherine "Kit" Foster for its own sake. For the chance to do something of her own choice.

Katabasis: a going down, a descent to the underworld. Most stories of katabasis end badly. But Wasp's katabasis is at the same time her coming-of-age, her discovery of who she is when she has the opportunity to make her own choices. And for both Wasp and the ghost—who has forgotten his own name, as Wasp has almost forgotten who she was before she was Wasp—the going-down is also a going-back: as the ghost leads Wasp through the underworld, Wasp enters the memories of Kit Foster, and sees part of their lives—Foster's and the ghost's—as supersoldiers created for war, before the apocalypse that left the world as Wasp knows it.

I feel it is important to mention that *Archivist Wasp* eschews romantic cliché entirely. There is no romance. This makes the novel all the more powerful.

Archivist Wasp has great strength of voice. (The strength of voice and the mix of magic and technology in the worldbuilding put me in mind of another novel from the last couple of years, in fact. If you enjoyed Karina Sumner-Smith's *Radiant*, you will love this. And *vice versa*, I can all but guarantee it.) It has really compelling characters: Wasp, prickly and desperate, fierce and bitter but still with a core of compassion; the ghost; Foster (oh, heavens, Foster). The other girls, some of whom are never named. (The ending. Oh, the ending.) And it brings what should be disparate parts together into a startling unity, an imaginative whole that rips a small place open inside me and fills it up with feelings.

In short: *ARCHIVIST WASP*. YES. READ IT. YES.

It really is very good.

Seth Dickinson, *The Traitor Baru Cormorant*
Not-a-review: lizbourke.wordpress.com, July 22, 2015

This is not a review. For this to be a proper review, I would have had to read *The Traitor Baru Cormorant* (2015) thoroughly, in its entirety, from cover to cover—and for the second time, my will has failed in that regard. (For the second time, I skipped ahead to the end: some part of me hoped that the end had changed in the intervening time. Alas, no.) What this is, then, is an explanation of some of my problems with *The Traitor Baru Cormorant*: the reasons, as it were, for my intense and visceral dislike of this novel, even as I admire its technical accomplishments.

Look. Not every book is for every reader. And some books that *some* people will find powerful and moving and important will leave other people cold and alienated, or pissed off, or just unmoved. Ken Liu's *The Grace of Kings* (2015) is a perfect example of this for me: I can see the ways in which it is assured to be an important and moving book for other people, but I bounced off it within 100 pages. This is by way of an important preface to the visceral dislike that follows: I'm not arguing that Dickinson's book is shit and no one should read it. I'm saying that it pissed *me* off in a very subjective, personal way.

Now, for the book.

Let me enumerate, first, *The Traitor Baru Cormorant*'s good points. (It's important to be fair. I am trying very hard to be fair.) On a technical level, it is really very good: Dickinson's prose is crisp, he has a good eye for pace and character, and a knack for getting a great deal across with an economy of description. Structurally, too, this is a cunning, clever novel, with a nested series of deceptions and betrayals at its heart, crux, and climax. It's a story about imperialism, about politics, about colonialism, and its main character is a queer woman (a queer brown woman). I so very much wanted to like it. Hell, I wanted to love it: epic fantasy with more queer women is a theme I occasionally yell upon.

Unfortunately, there's a difference between stories about amazing queer characters doing awesome epic things, and stories in which amazing queer characters basically exist to SUFFER for BEING QUEER.

Warning: this will likely degenerate into ranting. With caps. Also, spoilers.

So, the Masquerade. Dickinson's Masked Empire, the empire ruled from Falcrest. It annoys me. I am annoyed at it. It is a Very Colonial Empire. And it's a cop-out on actually interrogating empire and colonialism, because by any reasonable modern standard it's Pretty Awful. I mean, eugenics, Stasi-like levels of social surveillance and control, really intense homophobic repression, willingness to take advantage of diseases introduced to colonial populations, residential schools—pick two. Or three. All five is beating the really big drum of Bad Empire Is Bad.

Then couple this with an in-universe justification for imperialism that essentially boils down to But Science And Sewers, a justification no one really challenges, making it seem as though the narrative agrees that empire *might* actually really be okay as long as it's not *that* bad?

Hi. My name is Liz. I'm annoyed now.

I'm only going to get more annoyed.

Because in addition, this? This is a straight person's story about a queer person. The titular Baru's queerness basically exists in order to give her an axis upon which To Be Oppressed. There are no queer communities after Baru is removed from her natal community in the first chapter; no portrayed community resistance to queerness as a site of social control and punishment; no connections between queer characters bar Baru and the woman who eventually becomes her lover. It's all BAD SHIT HAPPENS and also GRAND HIGH QUEER TRAGEDY.

And speaking as someone who's recently been growing into the realization that she is in fact pretty queer, I'm really inclined to be pissed when I'm offered the story of an awesome queer character—and it turns out, right, it turns out that this is the ANTITHESIS of the coming-out story. This is the closet or DEATH story. Actually, *both*.

CLOSET AND DEATH.

So to speak.

Let's dogleg back to the problem of empire for a moment, on the way to more yelling about the book's queer stuff.

So, right. I'm Irish. (Bear with me, there's a point coming.) In many ways this gives me a peculiar view of colonial empires. And of colonialism and imperialism—both beneficiary, and on the other hand, have you *looked* at Irish history? (And the myths we tell about Irish history, too.) And it seems to me that Dickinson is in some ways writing a *message* book. A book about how EMPIRE IS BAD and HOMOPHOBIA IS BAD…and not really grasping, on more than a superficial intellectual level, the ways in which people accommodate and resist *at the same time and with the same tools*. And that this applies as much to social repression as it does to the colonization of identities.

Dickinson might theoretically get the idea of the "colonization of the mind" but he misses the doubled vision that's the eternal gift and legacy of colonial empires to their possessions and the people thereof. That's the poisoned chalice pressed upon subaltern identities. And you know, he's *trying*. He's definitely *trying*. That he didn't get this right for me doesn't mean he didn't get it right for someone else!

But. But. The reason this is not a review is because of the middle bit. The middle bit that I've twice failed to do more than skim, where Baru leads a rebellion that it turns out was actually a mousetrap, falls in love, betrays the rebellion (because *layered* mousetrap), tries to save her lover, fails—

I did read the conclusion. The conclusion where Baru and her lover Tain Hu are reunited, Tain Hu a prisoner and Baru walking a political knife's edge. The conclusion where Baru condemns her lover to death so that the people who've been grooming Baru to become one of them (her some-time allies, her employers, the secret inner committee of the Falcrest imperial republic) cannot use either Tain Hu or the fact of Baru's queerness as leverage against her.

These are grand high tragic scenes, naturally. With mental swearing of ultimate vengeance on the forces that compel, COMPEL I SAY, Baru to do this thing. And Tain Hu? Tain Hu helps manipulate Baru into it, as one last strike against Falcrest—with her death, fighting for Baru's position on a political battlefield.

Fuck you. Seriously, fuck you.

When I was reading *The Traitor Baru Cormorant* for the first time, I reached the point where it becomes obvious that Baru and Tain Hu are liable to get involved. And I skipped ahead to the conclusion, because if experience has taught me one thing, it's that you really can't trust a mainstream book to not fuck over its queer characters. Especially queer women—and there are so few queer women protagonists in fantasy and science fiction. So damn few.

And I read the conclusion, and my reaction was *you did NOT just do that.*

And I went back and skimmed, to fill in the gaps. (Skimmed, because I drew the line at getting more emotionally invested than I had to be.) And Tain Hu is awesome. She's clever and honorable and courageous and true to her word, even unto death. And Baru is awesome: she's clever and tricksy and courageous and layered like a fucking onion (and all the layers have sharp edges), caught between everything she's already sacrificed to get this far and everything she's going to have to sacrifice to attain her ultimate goal—which is protect the people she was taken from back in chapter two.

And my visceral reaction? My visceral reaction was to fucking *cry* at the sheer bloody waste of it, because here, *here*, you have a mainstream epic fantasy that has two *epic* queer female characters, and you don't have the fucking grace to let them both walk away. No. Instead we get another iteration of Queer People Cannot Be Happy. Instead we get:

"I will paint you across history in the color of their blood." (Dickinson, 2015, 396)

Oh, it's effective. It's astonishingly well-written. In a way, that only makes it worse. If it were a badly constructed novel, ill-written and thoughtless, I would not have formed such hopes in the beginning.

Instead it feels thoughtless in quite a different way.

Chronicles of the Kencyrath by P.C. Hodgell

Review: First appearance

When first I read P.C. Hodgell's *God Stalk* (1982), the volume that begins her Chronicles of the Kencyrath series, what struck me most strongly was the sheer sense of *fun* that permeated Hodgell's narrative: a cock-eyed inventiveness that takes all the elements of sword and sorcery and makes them just that little bit *weirder*.

Just that little bit more compelling.

The publication history of the Chronicles of the Kencyrath is a scattered, interrupted one. *God Stalk* came out in 1982, followed in 1985 by the sequel *The Dark of the Moon*. But it would be another nine years before the third volume, *Seeker's Mask* (1994), emerged from a different publishing house, and another twelve years before *To Ride a Rathorn*, the fourth book, came out from Meisha Merlin (in 2006, shortly before that publisher's collapse). The series finally found what seems to be its final home with Baen Books with the publication of the fifth book, *Bound in Blood*, in 2010, followed shortly thereafter by *Honor's Paradox* (2011) and in 2014, by *The Sea of Time*. Hodgell is presently, one is given to understand, under contract for a further two novels in the series.

I became aware of Hodgell's work soon after the publication of *To Ride a Rathorn*, when a friend went all joyfully enthusiastic on me. And I will always be grateful to that friend, because the Chronicles of the Kencyrath includes some of the best and most enjoyable fantasy novels I've ever read.

Not bad, for a series that opens looking like almost exactly the kind of fantasy Terry Pratchett parodied in *The Colour of Magic* (1983).

When it comes to these novels, I don't want to talk about what they *do* so much as what they mean to me. And that is a difficult thing to do, when so much of what they mean to me is bound up in inchoate thoughts about what fantasy is and what fantasy is *for*.

I have said elsewhere that I consider sword and sorcery to be the fantasy of encounter.[1] In sword & sorcery, the concerns are more quotidian than in high fantasy, the fantasy of politics and nations, and the "things numinous, strange, and threatening" are less *totalizing* than in epic fantasy. (For in epic fantasy, epic threat tends to overshadow every other element: struggles are epochal, overwhelming, all-consuming.)

Boundaries between these categories are, naturally, porous: the generic landscape of fantasy exists as a continuum. Very few hard divisions can be made. And yet series which start out with a decided affinity to one section of that continuum rarely grow to encompass others.

But the Chronicles of the Kencyrath series leaves an epic-level threat against the background, treats it in an *un*totalizing manner, and throws *weird* shit at its protagonists with very much a sword-and-sorcery tone. For the series opens with a young woman—Jame, short for Jamethiel—arriving, partially amnesiac, into the god-ridden city of Tai-tastigon. Jame is one of the Kencyrath, whose people have fought a losing war for millennia, from world to world, against the encroachment of a force called Perimal Darkling. The unhappy history of her people got even more unhappy when they were forced to flee to Rathillien, their present refuge: they were betrayed by their leader, Gerridon

---

1 "Sword & sorcery isn't defined by the quest, even when quests are taking place during it…it's defined more by its tension between quest/magic as a means of making a living (or as intrusions into regular means of making a living), and its encounters with things numinous, strange, and threatening." "Epic Fantasy is Crushingly Conservative?" this volume (p.176, note 3).

High Lord, who turned to the forces of darkness in search of eternal life and brought his wife and household with him.

Jame's father drove her out of his house while she was still a child, once she manifested traits that marked her as potentially close to the three-faced god of the Kencyrath. Her upbringing has been unusual, for she has spent some of it—not that she remembers it all—under the shadow of darkness. Her development over the series charts a course from the protagonist of a sword-and-sorcery novel into something much more complex and much more strange. In *God Stalk* she's haplessly catapulted into the middle of events while trailing accidental destruction in her wake: in *Dark of the Moon*, she makes a perilous journey pursued by enemies in order to return to her own people—and give her brother their father's sword and ring—while in *Seeker's Mask* she finds herself confined by the social expectations for a woman of her rank and lineage and achieves a path *out* of those expectations. Throughout these three novels, which form the first part of what bids fair to be a structural triptych, Jame learns more about the nature of both Rathillien and the threat posed by Perimal Darkling—and her potential role as one of the prophesied figures who might either save or destroy the Kencyrath and with them all of creation. The second part of the triptych—*To Ride a Rathorn, Bound In Blood,* and *Honor's Paradox*—sees Jame forced into a leadership role among students at the military academy of Tentir, learning more about the past of her lineage and the politics among the divided Kencyrath, while it looks like the third—beginning with 2014's *The Sea of Time*—will see Jame pushed into more significant confrontations with Perimal Darkling and its servants.

Jame breaks things. It's what she does. She's not a leader, except by dint of either accident or great effort—and she's not a particularly good leader. She trails destruction behind her like an honorable, well-meaning hurricane: although she does her best, *something* is always going to get damaged. And this delights me, because dear heaven, her flaws are so obvious, and the narrative acknowledges them, and yet she's not rendered either tragic or unheroic, and—although there's a great deal of sympathetic humor—she's never portrayed as *bumbling*. (Stumbling, sometimes. Often.)

And her role, caught between the Kencyrath and the native forces of Rathillien, a bridge between peoples/cultures/powers, is a fascinating one, and one that has been rarely developed in quite this manner in fantasy novels.

I have a great deal of affection for this series. I think it demonstrates the breadth of potential within the landscape of fantasy—both the landscape of epic, and the landscape of encounter—and does it without ever losing either a sense of humor or a humane touch.

Martha Wells' *The Element of Fire*

Sleeps With Monsters: Tor.com, April 16, 2013

Many critics, many *reviewers*, I think, find it difficult to talk plainly about the things that they love and the reasons why they love them. The temptation exists to direct your attention primarily to its flaws, to minimize or to justify the ways in which it falls short of objective perfection. (Not that objective perfection is a thing that exists, except theoretically.) It is possible to speak of flaws objectively, and of technique. Speaking of what you love and why you love it—speaking honestly—exposes yourself. It's a form of intellectual nakedness.

This lengthy preamble is my way of talking myself around to confronting Martha Wells' first novel, *The Element of Fire* (1993).

The Element of Fire is twenty years old this year (2013). It's one of the best books I've ever read, and I wonder how much more I would have loved it had I read it in my teens, before I developed the first smidgens of the analytical reflex. (I came to it relatively late.) It's Martha Wells' debut novel, and as a debut novel it is singularly accomplished. It situates itself at a remove from the faux-medievalism of high fantasy with which the rest of the field (at the time of its publication) was largely in dialogue, but, while second-world fantasy, it hasn't cut itself adrift from historical context: it has the flavor of *ancien régime* France while being wholly, entirely, its own thing.

The court of Ile-Rien, around which the action of *The Element of Fire* centers itself, is a complicated place. King Roland, recently come to his majority, is a weak ruler, warped by the abuse of his years-dead father. The court's real power remains the Dowager Queen, Ravenna, who retains authority despite having relinquished the regency. Thomas Boniface, Captain of the Queen's Guard and Ravenna's lover (and her favorite), has to navigate the dangerous personality politics of the court, between the king, his favorite (and cousin) Denzil, Ravenna, and the young queen. Not only this: a dangerous sorcerer, Urbain Grandier, seems to have arrived in town, and while Thomas succeeds in rescuing another sorcerer from his grasp, no one appears to have any idea what Grandier means to do next.

Into this web of tensions, Kade, called Kade Carrion, unexpectedly reappears. Roland's bastard elder sister, daughter of the old king and the fayre Queen of Air and Darkness (who abandoned her to the mercies of the court), she's well known to hate her family. What she really wants is a mystery to Thomas, and to the court. She could be in league with Grandier or mean to press her own claim on the throne. But when dark armies out of fayre attack the palace itself, Thomas at least must trust Kade—and Kade must trust Thomas.

Wells' deftness of characterization is delicate, precise, and astute. An outside attack doesn't lead to all the court's factions banding together under capable leadership: rather it intensifies the amount of politicking and the coming-to-fruition of treasonous plots. The characters, down to the least of them, are no blank placeholders. Wells has a fantastic touch for conjuring personality in all of her work, and here the characters of Kade and Thomas, particularly—Kade roguish, damaged, fey, and honorable in her own way; Thomas world-weary, cynical, and loyal where his loyalty is given—come alive in their interactions with their world.

I think it a fantastic book.

Martha Wells' *The Wizard Hunters*
Sleeps With Monsters: Tor.com, April 23, 2013

> Florian gestured in exasperation. "It's like you're two
> people. One of them is a flighty artist, and I like her.
> The other one is bloody-minded and ruthless and
> finds scary things funny, and I'm not sure I like her
> very much; but whenever we're about to die, she's
> the one who gets all three of us through it alive." She
> pressed her lips together, then asked seriously, "Which
> one are you? I'd really like to know." (Wells, 2003, 379)

We first meet Tremaine Valiarde in Wells' *The Wizard Hunters*
(2003) at nine o'clock at night, in a library, while she's trying to
find a way to kill herself "that would bring in a verdict of natural
causes in court." Tremaine is the daughter of Nicholas Valiarde,
who starred in *The Death of the Necromancer* (1998). This is the
same Ile-Rien of *The Element of Fire*, but centuries later, and now
it is menaced by a powerful, seemingly unstoppable enemy. The
Gardier came, it appears, from nowhere, with no intention but
conquest: the war has been going on for the last three years and
the Rienish are on the verge of being overrun. Tremaine is summoned out of her library by the sorcerer Gerard, because she possesses a magical sphere—made for her by her Uncle Aristide as
a child's plaything—that may be the key to Ile-Rien's last chance
to hold off the enemy. Dropped—in some cases literally—head-
first into danger, her stubborn, ruthless, and above all *loyal* streak
drives the other characters forward, time and time again.

> "When he was about to hit you. You just…watched
> him. It was creepy."
> "Well, yes," Tremaine had to admit. "I should have

flinched. It made him more suspicious when I didn't."
(Wells, 2003, 123)

It's been so long since I've reread The Fall of Ile-Rien trilogy that I've forgotten how it ends. *The Wizard Hunters* is actually the first of Wells' books I ever read, about eight years ago. I was a little too unformed in my tastes then to appreciate how well Wells brings disparate elements together and integrates them into the narrative. Not to mention her stellar prose and good pacing. Tone-perfect descriptions that don't get in their own way.

Tremaine, Gerard, the young sorcerer-in-training Florian, and an intelligence captain end up discovering where the Gardier have been coming from—a whole new world which they've been using as a staging post. This world already has its native inhabitants, and two of them, Ilias and Giliead, form the other half of the narrative—although soon enough, the two halves collide.

For Ilias and Gil and their people, wizards are evil. The only wizards they've ever known are emphatically Not Nice people. When they encounter Tremaine and company, there's a clash of cultures and some very interesting characterization.

Also, tension, chases through twisty caves, shipwrecks, captivity and escape, evil wizards, and airships blowing up. Not necessarily in that particular order.

I'll tell you three things I love about *The Wizard Hunters*. I love that Wells' Ile-Rien has changed since *The Element of Fire*: it's not technologically static, and now there are automatic firearms and motor vehicles and airships, and the atmosphere of wartime Vienne feels analogous to WWII Europe, with blackout curtains and telephones and rationing and periodicals having ceased production. I love Tremaine and how she's unsure of herself and bloody-minded all at once. I love the deft characterization of other characters, like Florian and Ilias and Gil. I love how all the *cool shit* comes together, cleverly, with meaning.

Wait, that's four things. Oh, well. I could keep going, but that'll do for now.

This is most emphatically the first book of a trilogy. While there's arc, and climax, and denouement, in many respects we're building up to book two. It's internally satisfying, but not complete in itself. And now I'm going to have to reread *The Ships of Air* and *The Gate of Gods*, because I can't remember what happens next, and I need to find out.

It's a great book. Trust me on this one.

Martha Wells' *Wheel of the Infinite*
Sleeps With Monsters: Tor.com, April 30, 2013

There are two ways I can go about writing this installment of the Sleeps With Monsters Martha Wells focus….

…No, wait, there's really only one way. Because I cannot pretend to be anything other than utterly in love with Wells' *Wheel of the Infinite,* her fourth novel. Originally published in 2000, by Eos (HarperCollins), I first read it in some dim, misty far-away past…possibly in my second year in college, so not *really* that long ago. I don't remember having such a strong positive reaction on my first reading, which explains why this is only the first time I've reread it since. Perhaps, like many things, it improves with time.

The protagonist of *Wheel of the Infinite,* Maskelle, is one of those Older Women whose scarcity in SFF I've remarked upon more than once. Maskelle is the Voice of the Adversary, a priestess of very high rank within the Celestial Empire. The Adversary is one of the ancestors, whose Voices provide guidance. A vision of disaster years ago caused Maskelle to rebel in order to keep the present Celestial Emperor—the child of her body—from the throne. But the vision proved false, her rebellion failed, and now she's an outcast. She hasn't heard the Adversary's voice in years, and using her priestly power draws dangerous spirits to her.

When the book opens, she has been summoned back to the Temple City of Duvalpore by the Empire's chief religious authority, in time for the end-of-year rite. Every year, the Wheel of the Infinite must be remade to ensure another year of peace and harmony for the Empire: every year, the fabric of the universe is rewoven, and the Wheel and the world are one. Any change in the Wheel produces a change in the world. But there is a darkness in the pattern of the Wheel. Every day the Voices of Ancestors remove it from the pattern, but it keeps returning.

It's up to Maskelle—with the aid of Rian, a foreign swordsman whom she rescued from a band of river raiders—to discover why this is happening and put a stop to it, before a cataclysm overtakes them.

Mind you, Maskelle's rather hampered in her task by the fact that there are a lot of people in Duvalpore who bear her a grudge. Politics, interfering with saving the world!

In many ways, *Wheel of the Infinite* brings *Paladin of Souls* (2003) very strongly to mind. While *Paladin*'s power is unmatched—by me—*Wheel* is a book interested in similar things, with some surprising convergences. Maskelle is, however, a character from the outset assured of her power—though not always of how she ought to use it.

> Maskelle looked around thoughtfully. She didn't think
> she could kill all of them, and she had taken an oath
> not to do that sort of thing anymore, but she thought
> she could manage a distraction. (Wells, 2000, 6)

One of ways in which *Wheel of the Infinite* surprised me— one of the things I had forgotten about it—is how Wells brings the cataclysm to fruition and resolves the world-altering threat. There's no vast battle, no out-thinking of the enemy: in fact, the enemy turns out to have been other than they'd believed all along. Maskelle and Rian, in their complicated partnership, put things right through luck, stubbornness, and endurance.

Also a certain amount of intelligence just to *get* that far.

I remain amused and delighted by the fact that the group of players with whom Maskelle is traveling are not merely scenery. They stick around until the end, important, engaging, and well-drawn as all Wells' characters are.

It's not a book about grand heroics and Killing People With Swords. But *Wheel of the Infinite* is a fascinating take on an epic-type story. And one I think I'll be rereading more regularly in the future.

Martha Wells' *Emilie and the Hollow World*

Sleeps With Monsters: Tor.com, May 7, 2013

Emilie and the Hollow World (2013) is Martha Wells' thirteenth and latest novel, hot off the presses from Angry Robot/Strange Chemistry. It's also Wells' first novel marketed to the YA demographic, and speaking personally, I was interested to see how Wells would approach a different audience.

She doesn't disappoint.

Emilie, the sixteen-year-old eponymous hero, has run away from home after an argument with her guardians. Her reasons are defensible; her forward planning skills, less so. When her plan to stow away on the steamship *Merry Bell* to reach her cousin goes awry (a small case of mistaken identity—mistaken for a thief), she finds herself on the wrong ship. The *Sovereign* has fought off attackers just in time to set out on its own journey, one which will take it out of the world Emilie knows…perhaps forever.

> Lord Engels turned to Emilie and demanded loudly, "Why shouldn't I throw you overboard?"
>
> Emilie folded her arms, skeptical. After all the shouting and turmoil at home, being threatened with a dire fate wasn't as shocking as it ought to have been. She said, coolly, "I suppose you should throw me overboard, if you don't mind being a murderer. I prefer being shot to being drowned, if I'm given a choice."
>
> Silence fell as Lord Engels was rendered momentarily speechless. (Wells, 2013, 46)

Miss Marlende and her friend Kenar have enlisted the aid of Lord Engels, nobleman and scientist, to rescue Miss Marlende's father, Professor Marlende. The professor took an airship down the mouth of a volcano, riding the aetheric currents to the world within the world—the Hollow World, whence Kenar has come, bearing word that the professor is stranded. Lord Engels' steamship intends to perform the same feat by a different route—and not only retrieve Professor Marlende, but thwart Lord Ivers, scientific rival to Marlende and Engels, whose rivalry has turned violent.

Emilie, in her own words, "a nosy foolish stowaway," is caught up in their quest. Kenar may be a native of the Hollow World, but the waters they've arrived in are as strange to him as they are to the upper-worlders. Flooded cities, carnivorous seaweed, and the politics of merpeople lie between them and Professor Merlende. Not to mention further run-ins with Lord Ivers, kidnappings, daring escapes, and a spot of fighting. Oh, and the *Sovereign* can't get home on its own anymore: the experimental engine that let it ride the aetheric currents down into the Hollow World is broken, and without Professor Merlende's expertise, it may not be possible to fix it....

In *Emilie and the Hollow World*, Wells has written the very model of a Boys' Adventure Story, one influenced by the Vernian tradition—with a nod to *Journey to the Centre of the Earth* in the shape of the volcano—but with a Girl in the adventuring role. This, on its own, isn't revolutionary, but Wells peoples Emilie's world with other interesting women: Miss Marlende, determined to bring her father and his research home; Rani, Kenar's partner, who's instrumental in helping Emilie escape from durance vile and stage a daring rescue of other prisoners; the queen of the merpeople and her attendants, whose intrigue draws the crew of the *Sovereign* into the middle of a war. And Emilie is the perfect Adventure hero: swept up by events, she's determined to make the most of them. As a YA novel, it's conspicuously lacking in angst and romantic triangles, and I love it all the better for it.

The youthful demographic that reads Rick Riordan and Tamora Pierce is the demographic this book was made for. But it was also made for *me*—because while *Emilie and the Hollow World* isn't as complex and nuanced as Wells' previous novels, it still bears the imprint of her skill with characterization and occasionally delightful turns of phrase.

Read it. Give it to your local twelve-year-olds. It's made of win.

An Engaging Adventure:
Emilie & the Sky World by Martha Wells
Review: Tor.com, February 11, 2014

Most of you are, I hope, already familiar with Martha Wells. (And if not, what are you all waiting for?) *Emilie and the Sky World* (2014) is her second book from YA imprint Strange Chemistry, a direct sequel to 2013's *Emilie and the Hollow World*.

Sky World picks up immediately where the *Hollow World* left off, on the doorstep of our eponymous protagonist Emilie's cousin's house. In this respect, it feels almost more like the second installment of a fast-paced television serial than the next novel in a series: don't expect much time here to catch your breath!

Now, instead of being a stowaway, Emilie is gainfully employed as assistant to Miss Marlende, a scientist in her own right and daughter to the scientist and adventurer Dr. Marlende. But her problems haven't ended with their return from the Hollow World. Indeed, she's about to be catapulted into a fresh adventure, for when her friend Daniel takes her to visit his old teacher, Professor Abindon, she warns them that she's seen something strange in her aetheric observations: a disruption in the aether current of the upper air. It transpires that this disruption is actually a vessel, which appears to be descending from some upper world in much the same way as the Marlendes and Lord Engal descended to the Hollow World. When Emilie's uncle Yeric tracks her down and threatens to drag her back home, Miss Marlende agrees that Emilie should join the airship expedition to investigate the strange vessel to keep her out from under his thumb.

So *she* doesn't need to stow away—not this time. No, this time the stowaway is her younger brother Efrain, who always took her uncle's side over hers when they were at home. His appearance aboard the airship embarrasses her, but she's given little time to dwell on old family wrongs. The strange vessel appears deserted, but the first members of the expedition to explore it fail to return. Emilie and Efrain go with the second party and rapidly find themselves mysteriously transported to a strange and perilous landscape. Emilie and Efrain rebuild the bonds of family as they navigate hostile castaways, invisible mind-controlling beings, and form an alliance with the last surviving crew-member of the vessel from the upper air, a nonhuman person with petals and stalks. There is kidnapping, and derring-do, and tense stand-offs, and last-minute rescues, and terrible revelations—in short, all the ingredients of an excellent adventure story.

There's an engaging…not simplicity, but *straightforwardness*, to Emilie's voice. She's a pragmatic and perceptive character, but—unlike most of the characters from the works Wells has written for an adult audience—there are no hidden layers or concealed agendas. (It was especially noticeable to me here, because the combination of airships and magic and traveling to strange places reminded me quite strongly of Wells' *The Wizard Hunters,* and one thing that Tremaine wasn't, as a character, was *straightforward.*) At times this makes the story seem suited to the more youthful end of the YA spectrum, but there's something purely *fun* about Emilie and her adventures: you'd have to be joyless and stuffy indeed to *not* be entertained.

There is one disappointing element: I'd hoped to see a little more of Emilie interacting with—and upending—her everyday world. I'd have liked to see some adventures in the halls of august scientific institutions, more trains and steamships and aetheric navigators. But alas, this time out I was to be disappointed. But perhaps, though, there may be more Emilie books—including at least one where the strangeness comes to *her.*

Emilie and the Sky World is a delightfully fun, fast read. I'd happily read a dozen more in this mold.

Kate Elliott's *King's Dragon*

Sleeps With Monsters: Tor.com, July 9, 2013

I first read *King's Dragon* (1997), the opening book in Kate Elliott's seven-volume epic fantasy sequence Crown of Stars, in the same year I started secondary school.

Returning to it after an interval of (give or take) thirteen years, I find an immense difference between my reactions as a thirteen-going-on-fourteen-year-old, and my reactions now, as an adult with more context for the genre. *King's Dragon* is a novel very much in conversation with its predecessors and peers. It's interesting to see it now as a very close contemporary of *A Game of Thrones* (1996), in dialogue with so many of the same things—though due to the nature of publishing, while *King's Dragon* succeeded *A Game of Thrones* chronologically, it's impossible that the one could have influenced the other.

King's Dragon's main characters are Liath, a young woman with a mysterious background and some connection to sorcery, and Alain, a young man favored by the Lady of Battles. The third and fourth characters who have a perspective on the action are Rosvita, a cleric and counselor of King Henry of Wendar and Varre, and Hanna, Liath's friend. But *King's Dragon* is the first novel in a seven-volume epic fantasy arc, and its *dramatis personae* are appropriately many: from King Henry himself and Prince Sanglant, his bastard eldest son, to Sabella, the half-sister whose rebellion against his rule is aided by the senior cleric—and sorceress—Antonia. While Alain marches unwillingly in Antonia's train, Liath finds herself in the city of Gent, besieged by the Eika from the north…and strongly attracted to Prince Sanglant.

In *King's Dragon*, Kate Elliott has built an authentically medieval world, whose lineal relation to our history shows in the careful thought given to the king's progress and his relation to his nobles; in the church of the Lord and Lady, its roots clearly owing much to Christianity and the early Greek church, with titles such as biscop and skopos; and in the lives of the ordinary people who are affected by the desires of the powerful and their wars—people like Liath and Alain.

For *King's Dragon* is not a happy fluffy fantasy. It is, in fact, as grittily realistic as anyone might wish. At fourteen, it was the first time I had come across *real* intimate violence and sexual coercion in SFF, the first time the villains hadn't been obvious, and wickedness swiftly condemned by everyone around the protagonists. From this distance, I can see that Elliott was engaged in shining a light on some of the things fantasy was still mostly inclined to gloss over: at fourteen, all I understood was that my reader-identification character was being abused by a monster.

It remained a very strong memory for me. I never finished reading Crown of Stars back then—I believe I was distracted by exams while waiting on the fifth book—and despite my best efforts to *read faster* I'm still only halfway through the series now. (Read it. If you like A Song of Ice and Fire, or even if you don't, read it.) What I was willing to read, to *see*, though, at the age of fourteen and now, has spurred me to think thoughts about the nature of reading experience and how it changes. Am I more prepared, as an adult, to read things that aren't in some sense wish-fulfilment? Is that the major difference between Young Adult as a category and everything else, the depth of the average reader's *self*-absorption? Or is it only me that's changed, and am I extrapolating from too small a data-set?

Because *King's Dragon* is so much more interesting a book to me now, both in its own right and in that I can see the things with which it's in dialogue. It has flaws and absences—Elliott's succeeding epic series present a much more diverse cast from the offing—but it's a mature, intelligent book.

And brutal. It—and its sequels—still affects me quite viscerally, even knowing what was coming. Even after thirteen years.

I lift my hat to you, Kate Elliott. I really do.

Kate Elliott's *Cold Steel*

Sleeps With Monsters: Tor.com, July 16, 2013

Kate Elliott began her Spiritwalker trilogy in 2010, with *Cold Magic*. *Cold Fire* followed in 2011, and now *Cold Steel* (2013) has arrived to crown the ensemble. Elliott's métier is epic fantasy, and her fantastic alternate Earth—from its glacier-shadowed Europa to the Taino-ruled Caribbean and the revolutionary free city of Expedition, to the realm of the spirit world as well—is built with great consistency and complexity.

We see this world through the first-person narration of Catherine ("Cat") Bell Barahel, daughter of the Master of the Wild Hunt and a female soldier (an "Amazon") in the army of Camjiata, the so-called Iberian Monster. Her cousin and foster-sister Beatrice ("Bee") Hassi Barahel is a seer who "walks the dreams of dragons," and people want to control her in order to make use of her visions. Her half-brother Rory is a shapeshifting giant cat. When the novel opens, Cat is still in the city of Expedition. Her husband, the cold mage Andevai Diarisso Haranwy, has been abducted by her father for nefarious purposes. And Bee's husband, Prince Caonobo, is bringing her to court to stand trial for the murder of his mother, the former Taino queen, or *cacica*, Anacaona.

And Camjiata, exiled from Europa years ago, is in Expedition, about to set sail for Iberia to restart his war to overthrow the old order, with the unscrupulous fire mage James Drake—who nurses a burning hatred for Andevai—in his train.

Cat is determined to rescue her husband. To do that, she must return to Europa—which she does, after some travails, through the spirit world, accompanied by Bee, Rory, and a talking skull holding the spirit of the *cacica* Anacaona. But her problems are only just beginning. Europa, divided by Camjiata's invasion, with the status quo of the privileged threatened by revolutionary movements, isn't a safe place for a wanted trio. Separated from Bee and Rory, Cat finds her way to Andevai's prison in the spirit world. But, having freed him from one kind of durance vile, she can't keep him free of the cold mage House that raised him from peonage, trained him, and refuses to relinquish the power his cold magic represents. Andevai is a vain, complicated man, and though he loves Cat and she him, that alone is not enough to conquer all difficulties. Andevai's mother and sisters and his own sense of duty are held hostage against him, and Cat eventually finds herself marching with Camjiata's army, while Andevai is ranged among Camjiata's enemies.

In the end, Cat finds herself calling upon her father, Master of the Wild Hunt, in a final bid to save Andevai and his cold mages from James Drake—and offering her own life in exchange.

The pacing, as in any 600-page novel, feels uneven at times. But in a sprawling epic that takes as its themes love, war, revolution, and people's right to self-determination, to freedom and dignity and autonomy, a little unevenness of pace is only to be expected. *Cold Steel*—indeed, the whole *Spiritwalker* trilogy—is one of a handful of epic fantasy novels that treats social change and social revolution thoughtfully, understanding the nature of a paradigm shift away from privilege (*privilegium*, private law) towards common law and equality before the law. Roman *rei vindicatio* is important not only in Europa, but in the spirit world, when Cat invokes it to claim possession of *herself* in the face of the blood-hungry powers of that realm.

Trolls. Dragons. (Dragons! Trolls!) There are battles and excellent action scenes and quiet tension and having the thing you most desired used against you. Daring rescues and rousing speeches, manipulative generals and complicated aristocrats and dashing—and not-so-dashing—revolutionaries.

Really, it's everything I could want in a book, and my big problem is that I want more of it more intensely. Not a longer book, but a sharper one: for all its Cool Shit (tm), I'm left with the feeling that Elliott has backed off from jabbing the point of her knife in the most effective places....

But not everyone enjoys being stabbed, and I do appreciate a happy ending, too. Go forth and read it: I suspect you'll have fun.

Reconfiguring Epic Fantasy:
Black Wolves by Kate Elliott
Review: Tor.com, November 3, 2015

I'm not sure that any review I write can do adequate justice to Kate Elliott's *Black Wolves* (2015). Here are the basic facts: it's the first book in a new series. It's set in the same continuity as her Crossroads trilogy (begun in 2007 with *Spirit Gate*), but several decades on, and with an entirely new cast of characters. It's out this month from Orbit. And it's the work of a writer who's reached a new peak in skill and talent, and has *things to say*.

On one level, this is good old-fashioned epic fantasy. A kingdom in turmoil; young men and young women in over their heads, secrets and lies and history, power struggles and magic and people who ride *giant eagles*. It has *cool shit*.

On another level, this is a deconstruction of epic fantasy. An *interrogation* of epic fantasy: it turns the staple tropes of the genre upside down and shakes them to see what falls out. It reconfigures the landscape of epic fantasy, because its emotional focus is not—despite initial impressions—on kingship and legitimacy, inheritance and royal restoration. So much of the epic fantasy field accepts the *a priori* legitimacy of monarchy—or the *a priori* legitimacy of power maintained through force—invests it with a kind of superstitious awe, that to find an epic fantasy novel willing to *intelligently* interrogate categories of power is a thing of joy.

Kate Elliott is very interested in power in *Black Wolves*. Kinds of power, and kinds of violence. Who has it, who uses it, who suffers from it, who pays the price for it—and how. Each of her five viewpoint characters are a lens through which we see power and violence play out from different perspectives: Kellas, a warrior and spy whom we first meet as a man of thirty, with his loyalty to his king just about to be challenged, and whom we see again later as a septuagenarian with a mission; Dannarah, the daughter of a king, whom we see first as a stubborn adolescent and meet later as a marshal among the giant-eagle-riders who serve the king's laws, a leader in her sixties with a complicated relationship to her royal nephew and greatnephews; Gil, a young nobleman from a disgraced family who must marry for money; Sarai, the young woman whose mother's disgrace means her family is willing to marry her to Gil; and Lifka, a young woman whose poor family adopted her as a child from among the captives brought back from war, and who comes into Dannarah's orbit when her father becomes the victim of royal injustice.

Elliott examines the role of violence, actual or implied, in the operation of power; and the role of power in the use of violence. *Black Wolves* is a book that looks at state violence, in the exaction of tax and tribute and the creation of an order that upholds the powerful; political violence, in the conflict between the king's wives over which of his children will inherit his throne; and the violence of cultural erasure, as the laws and customs of the Hundred are remade to better suit the desires of the king and his court and their foreign supporters. (*Black Wolves* is, too, a novel that's deeply interested in the effects and after-effects of colonization.)

For all this interest in violence, however, it is significant—and in some ways radical—that when we see sexual violence in the pages of this book, it is as a tool of punishment deployed by men against other men, and not against women. There is a near-complete absence of sexual violence and constraint directed against women. Indeed, Sarai's storyline includes consensual and mutually enjoyable relationships both with her former lover, the woman Elit, and with her present husband, Gil—though both of these are complicated by war, separation, and conflicting obligations. (I will confess to rooting for an eventual ending that lets them have a happy triad, if Elliott lets them all stay alive to the ultimate conclusion.) The women in *Black Wolves* are shown as not just having agency and influence, but having sexual agency—which the narrative doesn't diminish or punish. That's a choice that's still fairly uncommon in epic fantasy, and one that delights me.

Speaking of women! The women in *Black Wolves*, as well as having sexual agency, are shown as the primary political movers, even if living in seclusion like the king's first wife. Especially the older women. It is *their* choices that lead to major change—and major upheaval. And among the viewpoint characters, while Gil and Kellas are working to agendas outlined by others, Dannarah, Sarai, and Lifka are significant *independent* movers of change.

This is a novel about politics. It's politics all the way down. It's about families of blood and families of choice, families of chance, and family secrets and betrayals. It's about heritage and inheritance in all senses. It's also an argument about law, justice, and what happens on the edges of empire. It's about *consequences*.

All about consequences.

Also, it has giant fucking eagles.

I think it's brilliant. If it has one serious flaw, it's that it takes about a hundred pages (out of seven-hundred-odd) to really find its stride: the first hundred pages are set forty years before the next six hundred. Eventually, it becomes clear why Elliott made this choice, and how it works in looking back to the "Crossroads" trilogy and forward to what she's doing here: but it takes a little time before the reader's patience is rewarded.

But *damn* is patience rewarded. This is a really excellent epic, and I'm on tenterhooks to see what happens next.

Unfortunately, there's another year to wait....

Violette Malan's Wandering Mercenaries

Sleeps With Monsters: Tor.com, June 4, 2013

In the past, the Sleeps With Monsters column has debated the definitions of epic fantasy and sword and sorcery, its social orientation, and what Fantasy Has Done For Us Lately. Well, you know what fantasy has done for me lately? *Violette Malan.*

In the mists of history—or, well, not actually all that long ago—I scraped up the cash to go to World Fantasy in Calgary. When I was there, I found this book called *The Sleeping God* (2007), by Violette Malan. And stayed up too late reading it, naturally. This spring, I finally read the fourth, and so far, last published, in a series featuring the same main characters. The Dhulyn and Parno novels, as they're known, comprise *The Sleeping God, The Soldier King* (2008), *The Storm Witch* (2009), and *Path of the Sun* (2010). And, recently, after Kari Sperring pointed ed out to me in conversation that she saw Malan's Dhulyn and Parno novels as natural heirs to the sword and sorcery tradition in the vein of Fritz Leiber, I *knew* I had to talk about them here.

Because they're *fun.* Dhulyn and Parno are Mercenary Brothers, extremely well-trained professional warriors who hold to a stringent honor code. They're also Partners: lovers, shield-brothers, people who trust each other with more than their lives—but while this is important to their characters, and to the narrative, the books don't include a love story. It's a mature, solid *partnership.* And mature, equal, equitable relationships are rare enough in the fiction I've been reading in the last while that I feel obliged to congratulate Malan on this one.

What follows should not be construed as anything like a critical review. Instead, I'm giving in to my baser instincts and indulging in a bit of shameless cheerleading. Since I want *more books like these.* (Preferably more in the same series, but I'll settle for something near the same kind.)

The trend in fantasy in recent years has moved ever more towards the noir, the gritty, the grim. Indeed, if one may venture to compare architecture and literature, at times it seems like a kind of literary brutalism, a raw modernist reinterpretation of tradition. But sometimes you don't want to wade through gut wounds and detailed descriptions of blood, shit, and the horrible things humans do to one another to get to your entertainment. Sometimes, you want implausibly competent, fundamentally *decent* characters kicking ass and taking names, wandering the world and saving it—while, so they hope, getting paid.

> What God abandoned, these defended,
> And saved the sum of things for pay.
> —A.E. Housman, "Epitaph on an Army of
>   Mercenaries" (1917)

In all four books, the first one is the only one in which a threat to the world exists. This danger at first irritated me (being tired, then, of O WOES WORLD NEEDS SAVING), but now it strikes me as an apt melding of the genre conversation as fantasy subgenres: *The Sleeping God* is epic fantasy tied up in a sword and sorcery package. Or possibly S&S tied up in an epic fantasy package, depending on your point of view.

Dhulyn Wolfshead, called the Scholar, and Parno Lionsmane, called the Chanter, accept a commission to deliver the young woman Mar-eMar to her relatives in the city of Imrion. The political climate is disturbed, as a new religious sect is stirring up prejudice against magic-users, who come in four kinds: Finders, Menders, Healers, and Seers. Seers are the rarest of the lot: although Dhulyn herself is a Seer, her talents are erratic and all but useless—and she's the only Seer she's met in all her adult life.

Once they reach the city, complications arise. They find themselves in the middle of a conspiracy to overthrow the Tarkin, the ruler of Imrion, and Parno finds the family he'd thought he'd forsworn forever when he joined the Mercenary Brotherhood right in the thick of it—and willing to welcome him back. But the conspirators are being used by an even more sinister force, one that desires the unmaking of the world. And it's up to Dhulyn and Parno to stop it.

Well-rounded characters both male and female! Derring-do! Heroic (maybe-not-quite) last stands! Come one, come all....

In *The Soldier King,* our pair of mercenary heroes get into a spot of bother when, after a battle, they accept the surrender of a prisoner who turns out to be more important than he seems. In trouble with their employers for not handing him over as a bargaining piece, Dhulyn and Parno end up embroiled in another attempted coup—with a prince who'd rather be a playwright, and the last surviving daughter of a band of traveling players. Mages! Magic! Amnesia! A supporting female character who happens to be married to another woman!

The Storm Witch sees the pair traveling to a continent on the far side of the world from their normal haunts. Separated, each believes the other to be dead—and meanwhile there's an ambitious emperor trying to muscle his way out of his treaties with their clients, and a mage from a different time caught in the body of a princess and mucking with the weather. After that, *The Path of the Sun* brings back Mar-eMar and one of the secondary characters from *The Sleeping God,* the scholar Gundaron, and introduces a serial killer, another coup attempt, and alternate universes.

...I've been accused of incoherency when it comes to books I truly enjoy (I know, you're all *so very* not shocked), but trust me, the alternate universes make sense in context. Excellent adventure sense!

I've a very soft spot for sword-and-sorcery, the fantasy of encounter, that features a daring team of implausibly competent, decent people against the world. The Dhulyn and Parno books aren't perfect (what product of human endeavor is?) but they scratch a good few of my narrative itches in one go.

Nightmares and the Dark:
Barbara Hambly's Darwath Trilogy
Article: Tor.com, October 26, 2011

This year has seen the release of much of Barbara Hambly's out-of-print backlist in ebook format from Open Road Media. An exciting development for me: I'm young enough that some of these books were hard to find before I was even able to properly *read*. Yet, as an SFF reader, I'd heard nothing but praise for Hambly's work since I became aware it existed, and her in-print historical mysteries made a convincing argument that I would really enjoy her fantasy—if only I could find it.

So you can imagine how welcome I found the news that Hambly had released ebook versions of the likes of *Dragonsbane* (1985) and *The Ladies of Mandrigyn* (1984), amongst the greater part of her previously hard-to-find oeuvre. So welcome, in fact, that I simply *have* to tell you all about it.

I'm going to proceed in the general order of original publication. That means kicking off with *The Time of the Dark* (1982) and its two sequels, *The Walls of Air* (1983) and *The Armies of Daylight* (1983), the three original books of Hambly's Darwath series.

1982. I didn't exist yet. Margaret Thatcher had been Britain's Prime Minister for going on three years, the USSR was still a world power, and Ronald Reagan was President of the USA. (In case you're wondering, I had to look that last one up.) *Downbelow Station* (1981) won the Hugo, *Star Trek II: The Wrath of Khan* showed in cinemas, and Del Rey sent *The Time of the Dark* out into the world for the very first time.

It's a strong and atmospheric debut. In her dreams, graduate student Gil Patterson witnesses terror and panic in the nighttime cities of another world. When the wizard Ingold Inglorion crosses the void between worlds to follow her home, it becomes

clear her nightmares are not dreams at all. Ingold's home is menaced by the Dark, beings all but forgotten until they returned in
a welter of slaughter: the only hope for the Kingdom of Renwath lies in the ancestral memories of the House of Dare, whose
last surviving member, Prince Tir, is a child too young to speak.
Seeking refuge for this child, Ingold comes to Gil.

Things don't go smoothly, and before long Gil and Ingold—
joined by auto-mechanic Rudy Solis—are back in Ingold's world,
fighting against the extinction of the remnants of the realm. In
the course of a long, grim flight to the last place of safety, the
impenetrable Keep of Dare, Rudy becomes emotionally involved
with the young widowed queen, Gil becomes a warrior, and all
three are integrally involved in the politics of survival.

Hambly's characteristic precision of phrase and turn of description is present here, even so early in her career. From the
very beginning, the atmosphere is full of tension and dread.
The tone belongs almost to horror: not the loud, garish horror
of slasher films or serial killer thrillers, but the quiet, creeping,
pervasive terror of a cold-sweat nightmare. The creatures of the
Dark are both inimical and incomprehensible, and it's their ut-
ter alienness—as well as their relentless progress—that renders
them disturbing. (And I'm not ashamed to admit I got up to turn
all the lights on while I was reading.) The fact that there can be
no negotiation or compromise—not even *communication*—with
the Dark makes them more like a natural catastrophe than antagonists. "What can I say of the Dark, Gil?" Ingold says:

> What can I say that you don't know already? That
> they are the sharks of night? That they pull the flesh
> from the bones, or the blood from the flesh, or the
> soul and spirit from the living body and let it stumble
> mindlessly to an eventual death from starvation?
> That they ride the air in darkness, hunt in darkness,
> and that fire or light or even a good bright moon will

keep them away? Would that tell you what they are? (Chapter One)

More human antagonisms play out against the backdrop of the catastrophe of the Dark, of course. Everyone in the Kingdom of Renwath wants to survive, but Lord Alwir, the queen's brother, and the Church Bishop Govannin differ from Ingold Inglorion in their opinions both of the severity of the threat, and in how best survival is to be achieved. The politics and conflicts of personality established here continue in the next two installments, in which the Church's disapproval of things magical will come to play a greater role.

The Time of the Dark is part apocalypse story, and part—to borrow a phrase from Farah Mendlesohn's *Rhetorics of Fantasy* (2008)—portal fantasy. I'm a little surprised by how much more popular portal fantasy seems to have been in the eighties than it is today: it might merely be confirmation bias at work, but I can think of at least three other eighties-vintage portal fantasies (including Guy Gavriel Kay's *Fionavar Tapestry*), while I'm hard-pressed to name more than one from the last five years. In the case of the Darwath series, the juxtaposition of worlds and worldviews works very well. Gil and Rudy have unique perspectives on the Kingdom of Renwath and the Rising of the Dark, and in *The Walls of Air* and *The Armies of Daylight* these come even more to the fore.

The Walls of Air, now that I've read it a second time, strikes me strongly as a book about learning, and about apprenticeship. The survivors of *The Time of the Dark*'s desperate flight are holed up in the Keep of Dare. Outside, at night, the Dark wait. Inside, politics and claustrophobia form their own toxic atmosphere. Food is short. Refugees are arriving at the gates. In an attempt to find other wizards to help against the Dark, Ingold takes Rudy on a dangerous cross-country journey to the citadel of Quo, home of wizardry and learning. In the Keep, Gil and Queen Minalde must navigate the politics of subsistence and

Lord Alwir's determination to form an alliance with the armies of the southern power of Alketch in order to invade the Dark's underground nests.

The journey to Quo is also Rudy's journey of introduction into the disciplines of wizardry. Hambly's wizardry is very much a combination of vocation and talent: the desire to *know* for the sake of knowledge, a fascinating combination of a perpetual scientific curiosity and vast—if occasionally odd—understanding. This sense of *vocation* is common to wizards across all Hambly's early work. One might almost say it's their defining attribute, and I'll have more to say about it when I come to talk about the Silent Tower series.

In *The Walls of Air,* under Ingold's unbending tutelage, Rudy grows into his identity as a wizard. He grows, too, in his understanding of the world he's adopted as his own. In the wake of a terrible confrontation at Quo, a Rudy both more confident and more aware of his own limits emerges.

One of the most interesting things about *The Walls of Air* is how both Rudy's and Gil's previous lives inform their relationships to the new world in which they find themselves. Their experiences change them, but Gil is still a student of history, and the information she painstakingly collects from the few records which exist of the last time the Dark rose adds to the story's tension as Ingold and Rudy approach Quo.

The Armies of Daylight provides the conclusion to the trilogy. Alwir will have his way: the Keep of Dare and its allies *will* mount an invasion of the Nests of the Dark. But how successfully? For Gil's analysis of history suggests that, perhaps, the last time they rose, no human agency caused the Dark to eventually retreat again. Meanwhile, tensions continue to rise between Alwir and Bishop Govannin on the one hand, and Ingold, Rudy, and the wizards on the other, with Queen Minalde caught in the middle.

In terms of personal politics and what actually happens, it's probably the most complex story of the three: there are betrayals and reversals and some really unexpected developments, including the return of a character long believed dead. The tense atmosphere of cold, tense, creeping dread lasts right up until the final confrontation.

Which I'm not going to spoil, because if you haven't read the books and you intend to, knowing what happens with regard to the Dark in advance might wreck the fun. It would've ruined it for me.

The three books together form a very well-constructed trilogy. I'm particularly impressed by the way in which *The Walls of Air* fails to suffer from Middle Book Syndrome: it's as tense and nerve-wracking as the first and final volumes. These are damn good books. Why did they ever go out of print in the first place?

A final note on the ebooks themselves: They're generally well-laid out, but a small number of typos caught my eye, and—I don't know whether this was also true for original paper format—there are no section breaks within chapters, even at moments such as changes in point of view where one might expect them.

The thought occurred to me, after I wrote this review, that one could read a homily on the perils of climate change denialism into *The Armies of Daylight*. Or maybe I'm just strange that way?

Wizards, Warriors, and Women:
Barbara Hambly's Sun Wolf and Starhawk Series
Article: Tor.com, October 20, 2011

1984. Not a great year for global politics. In the U.K., a year-long miners' strike began, and the IRA attempted to assassinate Margaret Thatcher; in India, Prime Minister Indira Gandhi *was* successfully assassinated, while in Ethiopia, famine was responsible for the death of approximately one million people and the displacement of even more. On the upside, cosmonaut Svetlana Savitskaya became the first woman to perform a spacewalk, David Brin won the best novel Hugo for *Startide Rising*, and Hollywood gave the world *Conan the Destroyer.*

And Del Rey brought the opening volume of Barbara Hambly's Sun Wolf and Starhawk series to discerning bookshelves everywhere.

The Ladies of Mandrigyn and the succeeding volumes, *The Witches of Wenshar* (1987) and *The Dark Hand of Magic* (1990), can stand alone rather more successfully than, say, the Darwath series or *The Silent Tower* (1986) and *The Silicon Mage* (1988). Each book tells its own, relatively self-contained story, and that's just about my favorite type of series.

The Ladies of Mandrigyn's already been discussed on Tor.com,[2] so rather than mentioning what Jo Walton's already recapped, let's talk about a couple of things that made me practically *giddy* with happiness while I was reading it: first, the fact that it's deeply feminist, and second, the fact that this is definitely a martial artist's book.

2 http://www.tor.com/blogs/2011/01/dont-mess-with-magic-barbara-hamblys-the-ladies-of-mandrigyn.

To pursue the latter thought immediately: martial training forms a large part of Sun Wolf's story in Mandrigyn itself. Me, I'm a bad martial artist. I lack the discipline—and, quite frankly, the ambition—that takes a student past *average* to *good*. But I always enjoy stories that treat the hard parts of training with honesty and respect, and the Sun Wolf's training is all about the hard parts.

The main arc of the story bends around the Wolf, a "barbarian" mercenary kidnapped from his troop and compelled to train the women of the city-state of Mandrigyn to fight the forces of their local *really bad news* warlord-cum-wizard. But all the other significant personalities in this story are female. Whether that's Starhawk, the stern, solitary second-in-command of the troop, and Fawn, his concubine, who set out to find and rescue him, or the determined women of Mandrigyn—Sheera, their leader, the gladiator Denga Rey, Amber Eyes, the wizard-woman Yirth—they're a sheer pleasure to read. It's still rare to find a book with this many well-developed, diverse female characters—and not only that, but with well-developed female *friendships*, to boot.

There are two friendships in particular that brought this home to me. The relationship between Starhawk and Fawn is the first: the only thing they really have in common is loyalty to Sun Wolf, but Hambly suggests the development of genuine friendship during their journey.

The second relationship is that between Sheera and Drypettis Dru, friends from girlhood. They're both noblewomen of Mandrigyn, and the politics of their planned revolt brings strain to bear on their friendship, especially Sun Wolf's position and his training. But theirs is a recognizable, believable friendship, of the kind with which few fictional women seem to come equipped.

Female friendship has a much smaller role to play in subsequent books. While there's no dearth of strong women in *The Witches of Wenshar*, *The Dark Hand of Magic* has far fewer. *The Ladies of Mandrigyn* has an exceptional number of interconnected women, and I have to say, I find that refreshing.

I'm ambivalent about how the relationship between Sun Wolf and Starhawk is handled in *The Ladies of Mandrigyn*. Starhawk is steadfast beyond reason, this is true, but in a book with so many female characters it's a little disappointing to find that the emotional arc of the woman with point of *view* revolves around a man. (As does, for that matter, Sheera's—at least to a degree.) I'm probably unreasonably peevish about that, since I'm reading nigh to two decades later and may have been over-sensitized to Narrative Subordination of Women.[3]

The Witches of Wenshar (1987) does much to even the scales between Sun Wolf and Starhawk. This volume takes place in the kingdom of Wenshar. The city of Pardle Sho lies on the edge of the K'Chin Desert. Starhawk and the Wolf are there to seek someone who can help the Wolf learn more about his magic, but their stay is complicated by magical murders, demons, the politics of the royal household, and the king's daughter's betrothal to a lord of the shirdar, the people of the desert, who once possessed the kingdom of Wenshar themselves. There's a deserted, haunted city in the dunes; the remnants of really old, really *bad* magic; politics and infatuations, betrayals and desperate confrontations.

The word I keep falling back on to describe Hambly's books is *atmospheric*. I've said it about *The Time of the Dark*, and it's no less true for *Dragonsbane*, or *Those Who Hunt the Night*. It's very true here. The dead city of Wenshar is intensely creepy, and the demons who dwell there disturbing in the extreme, as is the revelation of who, precisely, is responsible for the murders—for which Sun Wolf had got himself blamed.

The Dark Hand of Magic (1990) is a book I don't like very much. I admire it immensely: viewed on technical grounds, it's a good, solid, well-written (and yes, atmospheric) book. Sun Wolf and Starhawk return to the Wolf's old mercenary troop, who have

3 You will probably agree that it's a little contradictory of me to both praise the book's feminism and gripe about its feminism not going far enough. Fair enough. It *is* contradictory, but I think I'm allowed to entertain two contradictory thoughts at the same time.

been beset by the worst luck imaginable while besieging a city as part of forces hired by the financial powerhouse of Kwest Mralwe. A wizard's work, the troop thinks, and the Wolf, though hardly trained, is the only wizard they know who might be able to help.

Everything, of course, goes horribly wrong. To describe all the many ways in which things go wrong for our heroes in and around the siege—and later the troop's trek back to winter quarters—would doubtless strain both your patience and my ability to refrain from too many spoilers, but there's no way around it. It's not a very uplifting book.

It's a book about siege, and sack, and a long slog north homeward through mud; about the breakdown of discipline in a mercenary troop, a wizard looking for a power base, and people being people. The characters are understandable, sympathetic, occasionally vile, and frequently do or suffer quite terrible things, and while the general atmospheric of bleakness is believable— even logical—after a while the cumulative grimness gets a little hard to bear.

Despite all that, *The Dark Hand of Magic* ends on an optimistic note, one that makes me regret the fact that it's the last published adventure of Sun Wolf and Starhawk. They're fascinating characters who occupy an interesting world. They would fit well, I think, in today's fantasy subgenre of Dark and Gritty: for although the Sun Wolf and Starhawk books lack the hypermasculinity so often characteristic of that particular subgenre, they are, it must be said, extremely good.

Summerless Years and Strange Wizardries:
Barbara Hambly's *Mother of Winter* and *Icefalcon's Quest*
Review: Tor.com, November 1, 2011

Mother of Winter (1996) and *Icefalcon's Quest* (1998) are two further installments in the Darwath series. They're essentially standalone novels, taking place sometime after the events of the initial trilogy. And while I didn't read them as ebooks, if it weren't for having read the first three ebooks, I would never have been moved to track this pair down in my friendly local copyright library. (Both *Mother of Winter* and *Icefalcon's Quest* appear to be out of print and hard to find. This saddens me, since from where I stand now, the Darwath series is quite possibly my favorite of all Hambly's fantasies.)

Tracking them down in the library was, it turns out, an excellent decision. *Mother of Winter* and *Icefalcon's Quest* are books from a writer at the peak of her powers.

I have complicated feelings about *Mother of Winter*. Gil, Rudy, Ingold, and Minalde are once again the major protagonists, but—even compared to *The Time of the Dark*—*Mother of Winter* is a book full of coldness, bleakness, and desperation.

Five years after the Rising of the Dark, the world is growing colder. Hunger is a constant threat at the Keep of Dare, for crops are affected not only by the weather but also by a bizarre fungus called slunch. Animals who eat the slunch are changed in strange and dangerous ways. When they start attacking wizards, Ingold and Gil set out on a perilous journey to the south, to the mountain known as the Mother of Winter and the dangerous, alien wizards beneath it who seek to remake the world in the image of the thing they guard. Meanwhile, left behind in the Keep, Rudy and Queen Minalde must deal with the business of survival: as Rudy helps Minalde and young Prince Tir investigate the secrets of the Keep's long-forgotten past and attempts to train another young wizard, he discovers that the worst threats to their survival may not, in fact, be kept out by the Keep's walls.

There is a *lot* of tension in *Mother of Winter*. The divisions inside the Keep and the connection between slunch and the cold; the dread of constant winter and the tensions between characters. After an attack by one of the slunch creatures, Gil finds that she cannot trust herself, for sudden irrational impulses tell her that she should kill Ingold; Rudy's young apprentice hates him and is convinced he's holding her back out of jealousy. Queen Minalde is pregnant and Rudy fears his skill at wizardry and medicine will not be sufficient for the birth; in the south, far from allies, Ingold and Gil must confront old adversaries as well as the frankly terrifying Mother of Winter.

Hambly evokes the constant atmosphere of cold, worry, and hunger with a deft touch. When Rudy begins to investigate the mysterious Saint Bounty and the area of the Keep known as the fifth level north, things become *really* creepy:

> Rats and insects went scuttling, but the grating sense
> of being watched, of being listened for, did not lessen;
> the sense that something dreadful was about to
> happen abated not one whit…. (176)

It's this creepiness, the constant, sinister dread, that gives me mixed feelings about *Mother of Winter*. It's a smart book, clever, emotionally satisfying and immensely well-written—but reading it made my stomach tie itself in knots. (From this you may gather that I have more adrenaline than is really good for me, and also that I'm not really the world's biggest fan of acid indigestion.)

Icefalcon's Quest has less creepiness—or, at least, its creepiness affected me less. It takes place two years after the events of *Mother of Winter*. This time neither Rudy nor Gil play the starring role: the story focuses on Prince Tir and the Icefalcon, a White Raider and probably the most deadly man in Keep of

Dare, if we leave Ingold aside—Ingold Inglorion being a wizard, and thus in an entirely different category of badassery.

When the Icefalcon rescues a pair of travelers who go on to kidnap Prince Tir, he holds himself responsible and sets out in pursuit. His journey will lead him back into the territory of White Raiders and towards the people he left years before, including his sister, the shaman Cold Death. While Tir is being dragged north by a wizard with strange, old magic for the sake of his ancestral memories, the armies of Alketch besiege the Keep of Dare. The final confrontation takes place at an ancient, haunted Keep under the ice in the north, and is full of very agreeable quantities of fire, blood, violence, and upheaval.

As the title implies, this is very much Icefalcon's book. As his pursuit of Tir's kidnappers leads him further north, we learn more about the White Raiders and Icefalcon's people, the Talking Stars People: about what brought him from the "Real World" of the north, where agriculture and building are despised as extraneous to survival, and where a moment's inattention can mean painful death, to the "mud-diggers" of the civilized south before the Rising of the Dark. And Icefalcon comes to realize—if not to admit—that the south has changed him.

The White Raiders are one of the most fascinating parts of the story. Hambly sketches a complex culture, filled with complex individuals, from Icefalcon himself and his sister Cold Death, to Icefalcon's enemy/ally Loses His Way. For the first time, we get to see the world of Darwath almost wholly from the perspective of people native to it, and it makes a pleasant change of focus. Tir is a very believable boy, albeit one whose life is complicated by the memories he's inherited from his ancestors; the Icefalcon is—well, he's the Icefalcon, and rather defies my ability to easily describe.

One of the things that I've noticed over the course of the Darwath books is how Hambly integrates magic with technology, conceptually. In a sense, the landscape of the Darwath books is doubly post-apocalyptic, because so much knowledge was lost or destroyed after the *first* Rising of the Dark. Magic is an integral part of development over time, historically and culturally, and it's a seamless part of the worldbuilding. Without that already-laid foundation, the magical technology which Tir's abductors now control—unearthed from somewhere—might seem to come a little out of nowhere. (I freely admit that the fact that the Most Annoying Character from *The Time of the Dark* returns yet again here annoys me, which might be affecting my judgment.)

(He's a very believable antagonist, but Mister Ego irritates me just about as much as his real-life equivalents do. Which is a lot.)

Icefalcon's Quest is the last of the books in the Darwath series, though there is—so I hear; I haven't read it— "Pretty Polly," a further short story available for purchase from Hambly's website. While it leaves the possibility of more stories open, it remains a satisfying conclusion.

"You don't happen to have a hacksaw about you, do you, my dear?" Barbara Hambly's Windrose Chronicles

Review: Tor.com, November 15, 2011

Are you feeling old today? How about young? *The Silent Tower* was published in 1986, which makes it just about as old as I am. It opened a new series for Barbara Hambly, the Windrose Chronicles, which would go on to consist of *The Silent Tower*'s direct sequel, *The Silicon Mage* (1988); and *Dog Wizard* (1993), which has many of the same characters but a different villain and a different focus. *Stranger at the Wedding* (1994; UK title *Sorcerer's Ward*), though set in the same universe, is essentially a standalone novel with completely different characters, and I won't be talking about it here.

So, 1986. That would be the United Nations' so-called "International Year of Peace." The year of Metallica's *Master of Puppets* album and the *Challenger* disaster. In April, the US carried out air raids in Libya in retaliation for the bombing of a discotheque in Berlin, while in November the Iran-Contra affair started to break. *Ender's Game* (1985) won the Hugo for Best Novel and *Labyrinth* and *Highlander* hit cinema screens; a computer with 20Mb of hard disk drive space was top of the line, and the Internet didn't really exist yet.

This last point is relevant because *The Silent Tower* features Joanna Sheraton, a computer programmer at the San Serano Aerospace Complex, in addition to the young swordsman Caris, the mad wizard Antryg Windrose, and a dark and terrible threat made possible by the combination of magic and IT.

It's another portal fantasy. This time it's a portal fantasy that opens with point-of-view characters on both sides of the multiverse divide: in California, Joanna Sheraton, who feels that there's something bizarrely wrong in her workspace late at night; and in the other world, Caris, who witnesses a murderer come through the Void between universes. Joanna's part of the story opens slowly by contrast with Caris's, but soon both of them are entangled with the wizard Antryg, who is allegedly both mad and dangerous and quite possibly responsible not only for the disappearance of Caris's grandfather, but also for Joanna's abduction from Earth. Circumstances may force them to work together, but over everything they do hangs the threat of mutual betrayal and the specter of Antryg's former master—Suraklin, the Dark Mage.

I don't really like *The Silent Tower*. Of all Hambly's books—at least, those that I've read so far—it's the one I like least. I'm not sure whether I feel this way because neither Joanna nor Caris strike me with any outstanding sympathy, whether it's because I just want to read about Antryg—who, for all his protestations of madness, strikes me as a supremely well-adjusted sort of bloke for a man with his life—or whether it's because the melding of technology and magic hasn't aged particularly well.

Possibly it's because *The Silent Tower*, for all its many wonderful turns of phrase and the interesting economics of its worldbuilding—Joanna travels to a world with early modern technology, where wizards are forbidden by law from interfering in human affairs and both the Council of Wizards and the Church wait to enforce the penalties (the Church with Inquisitorial cruelty)—is a little aimless: I have very little sense of the direction and arc of the story, despite having read it twice.

And I really don't like all the personal betrayals. Especially the final one.

From my point of view, *The Silicon Mage* is a lot better. Both Joanna and Caris have grown as characters and have more interesting goals. During the course of the book, they even grow some more. There's an actual, visible antagonist! There's more Antryg! There's female friendship, in which *The Silent Tower* was sadly lacking, and a fascinating encounter in a temple with a transdimensional being who believes he is the Dead God.

The setup and final confrontation rely a little too much on the melding of magic and technology: 1980s computer technology, over fifteen years on, is a sadly jarring relic to someone who's never even seen a 5 1/4 inch floppy. But *The Silicon Mage* is a worthy book and just about makes up for my dislike of *The Silent Tower*: between the pair, they make a self-contained story.

Dog Wizard, though it rather relies on knowledge of the events of the first two, is better than either. At least, I like it significantly more.

Some time after the conclusion of *The Silicon Mage*, Antryg is living in exile with Joanna in Los Angeles. When she is kidnapped from her apartment by a stranger wearing the robes of a mage, Antryg permits himself to be drawn back home, into the affairs of the Council of Wizards, where he is under sentence of death.

Once in the wizards' Citadel, though, it seems that none of the wizards of the Council know what has become of Joanna. They want Antryg for more than to execute his delayed sentence: the Citadel is having a spot of bother, and with mysterious Gates opening in the Void between worlds, they can't afford to kill Antryg out of hand. He's the only wizard alive who really understands the Void, and the Council members are convinced that he must be the cause of their afflictions—or the only person who can solve the problem. Possibly both.

Dog Wizard is a fascinating book. Antryg must negotiate the politics of the Council, discover why the Gates are opening—and find a way to stop them—*and* find Joanna before everything goes to hell in a handbasket. The Citadel, particularly its Vaults, is atmospherically described, and the personalities of the Council are well-rounded and human. And the Dead God reappears, which made me very happy. I quite *like* the Dead God.

And *Dog Wizard* has a sense of humor, which is something that *The Silent Tower* and *The Silicon Mage* rather lacked. Caris and Joanna are very serious, even earnest, protagonists, but as a character, Antryg has a crooked sense of the world's ridiculousness even at the most nail-biting moments. He reminds me of Miles Vorkosigan, a little. Despite pronounced differences, both of them get their way as much by talking rings around everybody else as by anything else.

It's a tense and pacey book, and all in all, really well done. And the conclusion is something I never saw coming.

In the final sum, my mild dislike of *The Silent Tower* and less-than-enthusiastic enjoyment of *The Silicon Mage* can't detract in any way from the fact that I downright *love Dog Wizard*. So I'm rather glad I read all three and delighted that the existence of ebooks made it possible for me to do so.

Kidnapping in Rome:
Barbara Hambly's *Search the Seven Hills*
(originally published by St. Martin's Press
as *The Quirinal Hill Affair*)

Review: Tor.com, November 9, 2011

Nineteen eighty-three was, it appears, a busy year for Barbara Hambly. Joining the second and third volume of the Darwath trilogy, *The Quirinal Hill Affair* (retitled *Search the Seven Hills* for a brief reissue in 1987) appeared on the shelves of discerning bookshops.

And shortly thereafter, as far as I can tell, seems to have disappeared.

A shame, because *The Quirinal Hill Affair/Search the Seven Hills* is a truly excellent story. It's possible that I hold this opinion because *Search the Seven Hills* is a book that could have been especially *designed* to push all my geek buttons—but I don't think that's the only reason. *Search the Seven Hills* isn't a fantasy, but rather a historical mystery set in Trajan's Rome. It's the story of the philosopher Marcus, a young man of the senatorial class, and his drive to find out what's happened to the girl he loves after she's abducted from the street in front of her father's house.

Tullia Varria is betrothed to another man, but Marcus cares for her desperately, despite all the consolations of his philosophy. His search for her leads him into places extremely unsuitable for a philosopher of his class, and his growth as a result—as a man and as a philosopher—is one of the most interesting things about the book.

Search the Seven Hills is also a story about Christians, for Christians—who, according to the common wisdom of Rome in the second century CE, eat babies, despoil virgins, and commit the most outrageous sacrileges—are implicated in Tullia's abduction.

Hambly sketches with great skill the precarious position of a cult seen by the powerful as a religion of slaves, foreigners, and madmen. She doesn't neglect to show the incredible and contentious diversity of opinion within the early Christian community in Rome, either—if there's one thing every Roman and not a few early Christian authors agree on, it's that Christians argued as if the world depended on it. And Hambly's Christians don't stop arguing even in the cells of the praetorian guard:

> *"Your* priest?" rasped a man's voice, harsh and angry. "And what, pray, would *he* know about it, or you either, you ignorant bitch? The whole point of Christ's descent to this world was that he take on the appearance and substance of humanity. 'For the Word was made flesh and dwelt among us….'"

> "Now, wait a minute," chided another man. "You say, 'appearance,' but *our* priest has assured us that the entire meaning of the sacrifice of Calvary was that Christ take on the true nature of a human being. That he was, in fact, a man and not a god, at the time he died."

> "Your priest is a fool!" screamed a shriller voice. "Who consecrated him, anyway?"
> (Chapter V)

As someone who spent many a long college hour being quite baffled by the vehemence and frequency with which Donatists and Monophysites and Arrians and Docetists denounced each other as impious idiots, Hambly's Christians—both in their squabbles and in their loose-knit communal cohesion—strike me as delightfully plausible. And not only the Christians, but her grip of the details of Rome in the second century, not just telling details of city life, but things like the ethos of the senatorial class, the relationship between wealth and status, marriage and the Roman family, makes the setting immediately believable.

The characters, too, are real and believable. Particularly Marcus Silanus, in whose strained relationship with his father and family we see some of the less pleasant faces of Roman family life, and from whose point of view the story is told; the Praetorian centurion Arrius, who combines a certain brutal pragmatism with shrewd understanding; C. Sixtus Julianus, "an aristocrat of the most ancient traditions of a long-vanished republic, clean as a bleached bone, his plain tunic the color of raw wool and his short-clipped hair and beard fine as silk and whiter than sunlit snow," a former governor of Antioch with many secrets and keen powers of deduction; and the slaves of his household. Even minor characters are solidly drawn.

The search for Tullia Varria and her abductors is a tense one, with many reversals and red herrings, both for Marcus and for the reader. Enemies turn out to be allies and allies turn out to be enemies: the climax involves a night-time assault on a senatorial villa and a confrontation in a private lion pit. And—although the Classics geek in me cries out for more Roman stories like this one—I have to say that it's a very rewarding finish to an interesting, twisty mystery.

Kari Sperring, *The Grass King's Concubine*
Review: *Ideomancer*, September 1, 2012

"Humans," said Yelena wisely, "call everything not like
themselves magic."
"Humans are stupid," said Julana.
(Sperring, 2012, 15-16)

Aude is a young woman of wealth. When she was very young, she
saw a vision of a shining palace, a gleaming world that beckoned
her forward. The urge to discover where it is and why it calls to
her stays with her as she grows up and persists past her first face-
to-face encounters with the unfairness of life: the discovery that
she has money while other people do not, and that there seems
to be no particular reason why this is so. Spurred by the desire
to escape an unwanted husband, she elopes with army lieutenant
Jehan Favre and sets out to discover where her family's wealth
comes from. Her quest leads her in the end to the WorldBelow,
the realm of the Grass King, which has been devastated by some
inexplicable catastrophe. Kidnapped by the Grass King's last re-
maining servants, the powerful and frightening Cadre, separated
from Jehan, Aude is commanded to restore the WorldBelow or
pay a terrible forfeit.

Meanwhile, accompanied by a pair of shapeshifting ferret-
women who have their own agenda, Jehan follows after, determined to find the woman he loves. While Aude explores the
decaying halls of the Grass King's palace and suffers the whims
and factions of the Cadre, Jehan travels in a boat of stone across a
lake of moss and through a forest of crystalline rock, in a journey
fraught with its own dangers.

Kari Sperring's *The Grass King's Concubine* is a delightful
book. When I say *delightful*, I mean that it entirely delighted me.

And, by turns, impressed me: this slow, languorous novel succeeds in combining the tone of a fairytale with the movement of a Bildungsroman and a deep thematic interest in the interaction between progress and people, machine and myth—all the social forces that come together at the intersection between power and oppression.

Not everyone will enjoy this book, with its graceful prose and elegantly unhurried pace. The story develops with measured certainty, Aude's quest unfolding in the present in tandem with the revelation of how the WorldBelow came to its present disastrous state—shown from the perspective of the ferret-twins, the fitch-women Yelena and Jolana, exiled from the WorldBelow for their part in protecting the human Marcellan from the Grass King's wrath—which was a long time ago, by the standards of the human world. The Cadre blame Marcellan for the changes that have devastated their king's realm: the truth, it turns out, is rather more complicated.

In many ways this is a meditative novel, playfully serious, lucidly written, possessed of a fine talent for engaging with the numinous without losing sight of the quotidian. It is both *more* and *different* than I expected when I opened the first page. It was not, for me, in any sense predictable.

Sperring's debut novel, *Living With Ghosts* (2009), received much well-deserved praise. *The Grass King's Concubine* is different in both tone and texture, but more than lives up to its predecessor. An altogether stronger, better novel, it bodes well for Sperring's future efforts; I look forward with great anticipation to what she will do next.

First Rule: Do Not Interfere –
Sherwood Smith's *Banner of the Damned*

Review: Tor.com, April 4, 2012

Banner of the Damned (2012) is a damned good book.

I had to get that one pun out of the way first. To be honest, I didn't expect to like this particular big fat fantasy half as much as I did: my fancy for Sherwood Smith's work is an off-again on-again sort of thing. For me, her YA novels have proved mildly diverting, and while I enjoyed her Inda quartet (*Inda* [2007], *The Fox* [2008], *King's Shield* [2009], and *Treason's Shore* [2010]), I can't say I found them strongly memorable. And I came back to worry at *Coronets and Steel* (2010) and *Blood Spirits* (2011) like a broken tooth—you can't stop prodding at what doesn't fit, much as it hurts.

But *Banner* is different.

Banner of the Damned isn't the best epic fantasy I've read so far this year.[4] But it's certainly one of the more interesting fantasies of the epic sort to emerge in the last few years, in terms of what Smith has chosen to do.

Banner is set in the same world as Smith's Inda quartet, but four centuries later. It comes in at just under seven hundred pages of text and spans—as near as my rough calculation reckons—something over thirty-five years, although the majority of significant events take place inside a ten-year stretch. Another author might have taken twenty years and ten books to tell the same story: Smith does it in a single, self-contained volume.

To encompass any length of lived time within a single novel without losing the reader's attention takes skill. It requires

---

4 That honor goes to Elizabeth Bear's *Range of Ghosts* (which may be the best epic fantasy I've read so far in my life).

a compelling protagonist with a vivid voice, a master's control of pacing and tension, and—in the case of a novel rooted in first-person perspective—some tricks to illuminate what's going on (so to speak) back on the farm.

Emras, *Banner's* protagonist, is just such a character. When the novel opens, she's thirteen, a scribe-in-training in the land of Colend.

Or rather, when her defense testimony opens. For that's the conceit from which *Banner* hangs: that Emras is writing out her testimony, since she's on trial for her life. We don't learn the crime of which she stands accused until quite late in the book[5]—if we learned it any earlier, it would rob the proceedings of tension and disrupt the story's natural progression—but the conceit of a retrospective account permits our narrator to use, when appropriate, a longer perspective, and for Emras to pull back and refer to events from the standpoint of other characters.

Emras is dedicated to her idea—the scribes' idea—of the Peace, to keep which is their third rule. And to her work. She's earnest, determined, and loyal, even as the progression of time and events places strains on her loyalties. The story follows her as she matures and joins the staff of Princess Lasva of Colend, sister and heir presumptive to the queen. Colend is a court famous for its style, and Lasva, a princess renowned for her beauty. Politics and personal heartbreak combined result in her marriage to Ivandred, prince and heir to martial Marloven Hesea. When Lasva travels across a continent to Ivandred's home as his bride, Emras goes with her. But Marloven Hesea is viewed with suspicion by half the world as probably tainted by the magic of evil Norsunder. So Emras is charged, both by Colend's queen and by the Sartoran Council of Mages, to be on the watch for Norsundrian magic.

But Emras knows nothing about mages or magic. In warlike Marloven Hesea, home to a brutal and suspicious king, she finds a tutor. While Lasva tries to interject Colendi diplomacy

---

5 And by then, we understand that although she meant well, Emras isn't innocent.

into Marloven life, Emras begins to master magic herself, in contravention of the first rule of the scribes: *Do not interfere.* As her mastery progresses, she starts to suspect that all is not as it seems with her teacher. Norsunder, the evil beyond time, *is* at work in Marloven Hesea—just not in the way that anyone expects. Including Emras.

Cue explosions.

I have two small problems with *Banner of the Damned.* The pacing of the last quarter is on the uneven side, as for a time Emras retreats more and more from engagement with the world.[6] And the dénouement feels less like a conclusive wrapping-up than a trailing away of loose threads....

Which is, I suppose, true enough to life. We don't always get *certain* endings.

But I found *Banner* tremendously enjoyable, despite its flaws. Kudos to Smith for giving us a book with an asexual protagonist, in a world where absolutely no hay is made over one's sexual orientation or the number of one's lovers (as long as there are no vows of exclusivity) as long as the nobility make their treaty-marriages and bring forth treaty-heirs. That on its own is cheering: it's immensely refreshing to see characters being (at times relentlessly) sensible and practical about matters of love, lust, and marriage. The characters are interesting, believable, and well-drawn,[7] the politics—national and personal—compelling, and there's plenty of action and excitement to go around.

I liked *Banner of the Damned.* Quite a lot, in fact. So if you're looking for solid, interesting epic fantasy, I recommend it to you.

6 The pacing throughout is remarkably smooth for a book that spans so much time, but it's inevitably imperfect.

7 In a shocking twist, *Banner* is filled with women who talk to each other about things other than men. Be still, my beating heart.

The storm is coming:
The ghost wind, the poison wind –
Amanda Downum's *Kingdoms of Dust*

Review: Tor.com, February 23, 2012

Kingdoms of Dust (2012) is a book that enjoys playing with your expectations. If you come to its pages anticipating an interesting but fairly straightforward story of fantasy spies, like 2009's *The Drowning City*, or a twisty tale of murder and intrigue, like 2010's *The Bone Palace*, prepare for something differently satisfying. If you're drawn here for sweeping epic and confrontations with the forces of darkness....

Kingdoms of Dust has sweep and scope and conflict. It never happens in quite the way you expect. That's one of the greatest strengths here, in a book that is in many ways brilliantly successful: it undermines the mood and tropes of high fantasy while retaining its narrative structure.

Exiled from her home in Selafai after the conclusion of *The Bone Palace*, Isyllt Iskaldur, necromancer and spy, is unemployed and vulnerable. With her apprentice, the androgyne Moth, and her former colleague Adam, she finds herself trailed and threatened by competing factions of a secret organization within the empire of Assar.

As does Asheris al Seth, half-jinni sorcerer, intimate of the Assari empress, and Isyllt's friend—inasmuch as spies on opposite sides can be friends. Asheris recruits Isyllt to help him investigate the ghost wind that wreaked devastation on Assar's capital, Ta'ashlan, and the quiet men who know too many of his secrets. When Moth is kidnapped and Adam disappears, Isyllt and Asheris set out across the desert to the ruined city of Irim, and a confrontation with the "quiet men" of Qais and the terrible thing they keep there.

There's a sense here of things come full circle, of the same thematic concerns as were on display in *The Drowning City* seen from the perspective of characters a little older, a little wiser, a little more broken. They're nuanced: Nerium and Melantha, from whose point of view we see the inner workings of Quietus, the "quiet men," have good reasons for their actions. Melantha, in particular, is very like Isyllt. There are no easy choices here: one of the most telling moments in the novel is when Moth says to Isyllt of Melantha, when the latter is trying to recruit Moth and set her against Isyllt, *She's trying to turn me.*

> "Ah." [Isyllt's] tongue worked against the roof of her mouth until she could say the words lightly. "Is it working?"
>
> Moth's chin lifted, her eyes unreadable. "I don't know yet."
>
> Isyllt nodded. There was nothing else she could do. (236)

Kingdoms is a book that succeeds on multiple levels. Downum's craft is rock-solid, with an able control of narrative and sentence, direction and pacing. The prose is richly descriptive—at times perhaps a little much so, but for the most part lucid and occasionally gorgeous. The characters are complex, well-realized: they have inner lives and diverse, believable reasons for their actions. This is a book whose failings are much more things of taste, nuance, and tone than any shortfall of skill: like any work of art, it, too, is flawed.

Kingdoms, as I said, plays with the expectations of epic fantasy. It has world-changing stakes and the possibility of the end of the world, and a small band who might yet avert calamity. But it resists straightforward oppositions, good/bad, right/wrong. Tonally, thematically, this isn't the story of how Isyllt saves the world. It's the story of how Isyllt comes to terms with her failures and her betrayals and her grief for dead Kiril—and, incidentally, saves the world. It's not an especially cheerful book. But it is a triumphant one, both in terms of Isyllt's success and in terms of Downum's achievement as a writer.

And it is an achievement. Many a writer has stumbled on the hurdle of the third book, particularly if their second proved as mature and accomplished as Downum's *The Bone Palace*. *Kingdoms of Dust* doesn't surpass *The Bone Palace*. That would be hard to do. But it doesn't fall short, either.

Also, it has a manticore.

Kingdoms of Dust is a very good book. I enjoyed it a hell of lot, and I hope to see Isyllt and company return again. Soon.

Building Bridges: *The Goblin Emperor* by Katherine Addison

Review: Tor.com, February 20, 2014

It took me some time to begin writing this review. For some days after I read *The Goblin Emperor* (and I read it three times straight through in three days), I had to sit on the urge to open any discussion of this novel with CAPSLOCK EXCLAMATIONS OF ENTHUSIASM, continue the discussion with more such exclamations, and conclude with CAPSLOCK JOY.

As you can see, the urge hasn't *entirely* gone away.

Katherine Addison is the open pseudonym of Sarah Monette, author of The Doctrine of Labyrinths series and co-author, with Elizabeth Bear, of *A Companion to Wolves* (2007) and *The Tempering of Men* (2011). *The Goblin Emperor* is her first novel under this new name. It should be emphasized right up front that while the worldbuilding is every bit as detailed and baroque as her previous solo novels under her other name, the mood leans far less toward the noir than does The Doctrine of Labyrinths. The tone is overall much more hopeful, and the main character here far more *likable*, than in any of her previous novels.

That main character is Maia, last and least regarded of the sons of the emperor. Maia has spent his entire life in an impoverished sort of internal exile, more than half of it under the guardianship of a man who hates him. But the death of the emperor Varenechibel IV and his three elder sons in an airship crash means that Maia has inherited the empire—if he can avoid becoming the pawn of other players in his court.

And live out the year, especially since it transpires that the airship crash that killed Varenechibel and his sons was no accidental disaster. Maia might yet meet a similar fate.

The narrative unfolds mainly within the confines of the Untheileneise Court, lending *The Goblin Emperor* an enclosed, contained air. Maia comes to his inheritance a lonely young man, and the role of emperor isolates him further: he has had no training to rule, and his struggles to navigate the machinery of power, the paperwork, the personalities, the *responsibilities* of empire, form a large part of the story. He must make connections and alliances and bind the disparate parts of his empire—and his household—together in peace and security: it seems fitting from a thematic perspective that one of the projects with which he gets most interested is the construction of a bridge over the river that divides two regions of his empire, the Istandaärtha.

It is a deeply engrossing read—every time I open a page, I find I simply get drawn into the story (which has made looking up spellings for this review rather time-consuming)—but this is only partly because of Addison's excellent ability to turn a phrase. The sheer compelling *attractiveness* of Maia's character figures larger. Because Maia, however desperately unhappy and uncertain he may be, is a fundamentally *decent* person. His response to having been ignored by his father and to having been abused by his guardian is to be determined to do better. To be worthy of his power and his responsibilities. To refuse cruelty and caprice.

"In our innermost and secret heart, which you ask us to bare to you, we wish to banish them as we were banished, to a cold and lonely house, in the charge of a man who hated us. And we wish them trapped there as we were trapped."

"You consider that unjust, Serenity?"

"We consider it cruel," Maia said. "And we do not think that cruelty is ever just." (Addison, 2014, 319)

Addison's worldbuilding is delightfully detailed and thorough. This is a world of printers and clockmakers, airships and opera and black powder and magic. There are intricate layers of rank and address and conventions of language, including a distinction between formal speech (the use of the formal plural *we*) and informal speech (*I, thou*). Fortunately a guide of sorts is provided in the form of an afterword, "Extracts from a Handbook for Travelers in the Elflands," and the aftermatter also includes *A Listing of Persons, Places, Things, and Gods*, which is rather helpful for keeping track. It all fits together, this complex mechanism of moving parts: it builds a world that *makes sense*, with nothing misplaced.

This is a book about survival, and betrayal, and friendship, and power, and strength. And it's a marvelously welcoming, readable one. A book you pick up and read when you're tired and sad, and all unexpected it's like being wrapped up in a comforting warm fuzzy blanket of glorious worldbuilding and shiny prose and decent people doing the best they know how.

The Goblin Emperor is the best fantasy I've read in quite some time. It's certainly my *favorite* of the last great while, and though it's early days yet, I suspect it may be the best single novel I read this year.

I vigorously recommend it, and I really hope that there's a sequel in the works. Because I desperately want to read more.

Mary Gentle, *The Black Opera*
A Novel of Operas, Volcanoes, and the Mind of God
Review: *Ideomancer*, June 1, 2012

> I have used the source material regarding the history and royalty of the Kingdom of the Two Sicilies with the same careful and exact attention to detail as the *bel canto* composers.
>
> Given that Gaetano Donizetti once set an opera in Liverpool and described it as "a small Alpine village outside London," the reader is probably safe in regarding *The Black Opera* as Alternate History.
>
> *The Black Opera*, Author's Foreword

Mary Gentle has a habit of writing books that get inside my skin and lodge there. Books full of sharp, glittering edges; books that leave me with catharsis and questions in about equal measure. *The Black Opera* (2012) is Gentle's first outing since 2006's *Ilario: The Lion's Eye*. An alternate history set in nineteenth-century Naples, *The Black Opera* showcases Gentle's deft hand with place and personality and her trademark blend of the skewily historical and the fantastically numinous.

In short, I liked it a lot.

The date is sometime in the 1820s. The place, Naples, in the Kingdom of the Two Sicilies. Conrad Scalese, atheist and opera librettist, is arrested by the Inquisition as a heretic after lightning strikes the opera house in which his opera opened. Rescued from the hands of the Holy Office by His Majesty Ferdinand Bourbon-Sicily, King of the Two Sicilies, Conrad's given an impossible job: write a libretto and act as impresario for an opera that must be produced within six weeks. A production that will be threatened and sabotaged every step of the way, and yet *must* go ahead. For in this world, music—whether in opera or the Sung Mass—is the conduit to miracle. And somewhere in Naples, a secret society known as the Prince's Men is organizing an opera to bring about a black miracle: to cause Vesuvius and the Campi Flegrei to erupt, a cataclysm resulting in the sacrifice of thousands—tens of thousands—of lives. And, by that sacrifice, to compel the attention of either God or the Devil.

Conrad's task is to write a counter-opera to cancel out the black opera, aimed at a counter-miracle: the last string in Ferdinand's bow if all other arrows fail. With Roberto Capiraso, the arrogant but talented Conte di Argente as his composer, and the resources of Naples at his disposal, the project seems possible, but Conrad's working relationship with Argente is complicated by the fact that il Conte is married to Leonora, the opera singer whom Conrad loved years ago in Venice and loves still.

I know nothing about opera, so when I say I found the scenes involving the entire rigmarole of an opera company vivid and convincing, I'm speaking from a place of ignorance. But the business of the opera is the heart of the book: Conrad's writing and re-writing and awkward-brilliant partnership with Argente, the squabbles of the company over who gets what lines, a glorious vivid culture of theatre—the haughty castrato soprano; Sabrine, fed up with playing breeches parts and enthusiastic for the chance to play *prima donna*; the insecure *second donna* whose reputation is trouble; JohnJack Spinelli, baritone typecast as operatic villain; Conrad's cross-dressing sister (and first violin and conductor) Isaura-Paulo, who wants to compose for commercial opera herself.

If the business of opera is the heart of the book, its soul is Conrad. Atheist, freethinker, natural philosopher: to him what the Church calls miracles are a part of the natural world with scientific explanation. The tension between faith and reason comes into its own in the climax, when in the shadow of an erupting Mt. Vesuvius, Conrad comes face to face with a miracle that could be called *god*.

Offset against and yet integral to the matter of the opera is the relationship triangle (resolved in a refreshingly unorthodox manner) between Conrad, Leonora, and Argente. It is here, I think, the book is at its weakest: both Conrad and Argente love Leonora with a passion that goes beyond reason. I don't feel that passion convincingly in the same way I feel the passion Gentle has brought out in Conrad's opera, *L'Altezza azteca*, *The Aztec Princess*. (But when it comes to the romantic passions, I'm a cynic.)

Gentle may call her work alternate history, but attractive as her gift for setting history off-kilter is, the fantasy elements here have their own magnetism. This nineteenth century hosts ghosts and religious miracles, and sometimes the dead return— conscious, in their own flesh, almost the person they were, and nearly immortal.

Gentle has a chiseled, muscular way with prose, and a vivid eye for image. The characters are real, alive, and individual. Her control of pace and tension is solid, masterful: the crescendo of the climax slides into a dénouement that, while comparatively long, *works* for me in a visceral fashion. The ending feels satisfying. It feels right.

I've enjoyed every book that Mary Gentle has so far written. *The Black Opera* may be her best work yet: tense, compelling, lucidly written, and arrestingly unafraid of the tensions at its heart.

Marie Brennan's *A Natural History of Dragons*
Review: Tor.com, January 8, 2013

> In this ancient and nearly forgotten age lie the modest
> origins of my immodest career: my childhood and my
> first foreign expedition, to the mountains of Vrystana.
> (Brennan, 2013, 10)

As a fan of the Onyx Court series and the intelligent, layered use
Brennan made of history there, I looked forward to reading *A
Natural History of Dragons* from the time I first heard it was to be
published. And it didn't disappoint me in the least—in fact, I'm
already pretty sure it'll be one of my favorite books of the year.

A Natural History of Dragons marks Brennan's first return to
novel-length, second-world fantasy since her second book. The
intervening years have seen a marked improvement in the quality and complexity of her writing: *A Natural History of Dragons*
is the work of a mature writer, confident in voice and execution.

It's voice that makes this book such a treat: the voice of Isabella Camherst, née Hendemore, a woman whose passion for
dragons and for natural philosophy begins—as we see—very
early in her girlhood, even though it is not precisely a respectable
pastime for a woman in Isabella's world.

Brennan seems to have modeled Isabella's homeland on late
Georgian/early Victorian England, a place with strongly defined
gender roles, country gentlemen whose families—particularly
daughters—are expected to be brought up to manners and an
arranged marriage, and where natural philosophy is a respectable hobby for gentlemen of means. The book begins in Isabella's
childhood, where her passion for natural history and dragons is
born after successfully preserving a dragon-like insect in vine-
gar. Childhood adventures and misadventures follow swiftly, and

very soon Isabella is an adult, married to one Jacob Camherst: a fortunate match, since Camherst shares Isabella's interests and is willing to share his library. Shortly thereafter, Isabella contrives to arrange for both Jacob and, against all propriety, herself, to join Lord Hilford's dragon-studying expedition to Vrystana.

Engaging thus far, it's here the novel really takes flight. The tone of a retrospective memoir permits Brennan to balance her youthful protagonist's ignorance and colonial arrogance with more mature reflection on the perspectives of the "backwards" Vrystani villagers around her. Brennan also captures effortlessly the enthusiasm for discovery, along with the long stretches of boredom and difficulty, that attends any scientific endeavor. Isabella's awe and enthusiasm for dragons are infectious, and the amount of thought Brennan's put into her worldbuilding is impressive. Only the top layers appear on the page, but it feels solid all the way down. There's depth: anyone looking for the chipboard behind the curtain will find realism instead.

But in addition to impressively well-thought-out worldbuilding and a compelling voice, *A Natural History of Dragons* has bandits, dragons that have mysteriously become far more aggressive than usual, dragon dissections, possibly supernatural goings-on, and intrigue. You mean, you *didn't* think there'd be intrigue? We're speaking of Marie Brennan, after all.

Isabella's relationship with her husband matures and deepens, as does her proficiency and ambitions as a dragon naturalist. At the same time, she has to deal with the villagers' fear that she's brought down a supernatural curse upon them for exploring some ruins nearby. When her investigations reveal a more mundane cause, the local lord invites the naturalizing party to stay with him, and Isabella stumbles over the source of the troubles plaguing the dragon-studying expedition....

I enjoyed this book a hell of a lot, but it's not perfect. Isabella acquires information by stumbling over it a bit too often for plausibility's sake: the coincidences that move the plot forward are a little too transparently coincidental in the aggregate than they are individually. But if I'm honest, I'd forgive far more flaws than this one in order to read about Isabella's adventures. In fact, for a character this interesting with a voice *this* engaging, I could forgive almost anything.

Luckily for me, there's not a lot to forgive. *A Natural History of Dragons* is a mellow and agreeable memoir, an absorbing and entertaining novel, and I want more.

Tell me there's a sequel.

A final note on the illustrations: Todd Lockwood has done a brilliant job with the book's handful of beautiful and utterly appropriate images. They're almost worth the price of admission alone.

Elizabeth Bear, *Range of Ghosts*
Review: *Ideomancer*, March 1, 2012

Better a storm crow than a carrion bird.
Range of Ghosts, Elizabeth Bear

Range of Ghosts (2012) is the epic fantasy you've been waiting for your whole life.

This is a grand claim, I admit. For me, it's a true one. When I finished *Range of Ghosts*, I felt as though an empty place inside me had at last been filled. Let me explain—no, let me sum up.

In the last decade and change, epic fantasy has rebelled against Tolkien and his inheritors, deeming world-saving quests lacking in realism. Bestselling epic today is dominated by ultra-grim hypermasculinism as typified by George R.R. Martin and Joe Abercrombie. The trend toward grim "realism" removes a lot of the element of wonder that makes fantasy fantastical, and—I say this in all love, as a historian—a constant diet of torture, rapine, murder, and unpleasantness is no more inherently realistic than soulmate dragons.

Range of Ghosts quietly sidesteps both Tolkien and Martin/Abercrombie and proceeds to do its own third thing. What it is doing is full of wonder, worldbuilding grandeur, and fantastic Cool Shit™—and also full of grit, emotional realism, and a light, ironic, humane sense of humor.

Temur is the grandson of the Great Khagan, who ruled the steppes from one end of the world to the other. Once, a hundred moons rose every evening with Mother Night into the steppes' Eternal Sky, one for each of the sons and grandsons of the Khagan. Now Temur is an exile, fleeing the conflagration of civil war, and his iron moon is one of a scant handful. When Edene, the woman who would be his wife, whose family's tents have taken him in, is abducted by the sorcerous allies of Temur's usurper cousin, honor demands he go after her. In a sense, everything that follows is Temur's coming of age. But if it's Temur's coming of age, it is also that of the much older Once-Princess Samarkar, now become the wizard Samarkar, who has chosen

> …to trade barrenness and the risk of death for the chance of strength. Real strength, not the mirror-caught power her father, his widow, her half-brothers, or her dead husband might have happened to shine her way.
>
> It seemed a small sacrifice. (Bear, 2012, 38)

Her path—her discovery of her power, and her accommodation with her new life—comes to run alongside Temur's. Joined by the tiger-woman Hrahima, they learn that a sect of the Uthman Scholar-God, the Rahazeen murder cult of the Nameless, is involved in the troubles that bedevil each of them, and in the war and upheaval that threaten all the nations along the Celadon Highway, from Messaline in the west to Song in the east. It is this sect, allied with Temur's cousin, which has abducted Edene. Temur and Samarkar's journey will lead them west, out from under the skies of their births, to the lands of the Uthman Caliphate—and even, perhaps, beyond.

Range of Ghosts has range and scope. Divine mediation is reflected in the sky: what gods your people follow—what gods have sovereignty over which lands—matters intensely, in an obvious but not intrusive fashion. Astrology, here, is less astronomy and more theology. It's metaphysical. And really cool.

The world is vast and expansive. The characters are excellent: well-drawn, diverse, eminently believable. There are flying rukhs and cursed cities, haunted tombs and the restless dead. Gripping tension. Bear's characteristic cut-glass prose. Powerful men. Strong women. Landscape.

I've nursed a secret love for vasty epic fantasy with maps since I began to read. It rarely finds worthy satisfaction. In *Range of Ghosts* it found more than satisfaction. It found fulfillment.

I recommend it wholeheartedly.

Shattered Pillars by Elizabeth Bear

Review: *Strange Horizons*, September 4, 2013

> The desert writhed with poison life.
> (*Shattered Pillars*, 2013, 1)

Honed and lustrous, *Shattered Pillars*'s prose cuts with knife-thrust sharpness. Too visceral and too pointed to call polished, the experience of reading it alternates between delight and painful intensity. *Shattered Pillars* needs to be taken in stages, despite its cresting pace, to absorb the impact of its language.

This is not a novel for those who prefer their prose self-effacing and unobtrusive, but for those who glory in a well-turned phrase.

> She glanced back, and the conquering wizard was
> gone, fallen into a proud woman with drawn cheeks
> and a sun squint beginning at the corners of her eyes.
>
> "It is true," she allowed. "You have got a problem." Then,
> conversationally: "Empires are filthy things, you know."
>
> He knew. He had grown up in the war camps and on
> the borders of one. And he knew, too, what happened
> when empires fell. "But are they so filthy as the lack of
> them?" (44)

If I speak of the language first, it is because it hits me hardest. On a second reading, and on a third, relieved of the urgent tension to know what comes next, it is the language that endures, that provides a new appreciation of nuance. That shows me something fresh and clean, or something rich and strange.

Shattered Pillars is beautifully written. Bear's usual chiseled prose has matured to greater heights, but her attention to language hasn't in the least altered her ability to write fully fleshed characters who live and breathe from the page.

The second volume of Hugo-Award-winning author Elizabeth Bear's Central Asia-inspired Eternal Sky trilogy, this novel follows 2012's *Range of Ghosts*, which I loved with a passion that surpasses rational bounds. *Range of Ghosts* was the epic fantasy I had waited all my life—unknowing, but waiting—to come home to. It set a very high bar, and on first reading, *Shattered Pillars* failed to live up to my expectations for a sequel.

But this is a book that rewards rereading.

Re Temur, grandson of the dead Khagan of the steppe, rider of the bay mare Bansh, and Samarkar-la, once-princess of Rasa, wizard of Tsarepheth, and Temur's lover, have come to the city of Asitaneh, seat of the Uthman Caliphate and home of Temur's maternal grandfather, Ato Tesefahun. They seek the Caliph's recognition for Temur's claim to the Khaganate and Ato Tesefahun's aid in rescuing Edene, the woman who carries Temur's child, from the Rahazeen cult of the Nameless. Who, unbeknownst to them, has already escaped, carrying a ring of power, to raise an army of ghulim in the desert of ancient, deadly Erem.

Several strands of narrative thread *Shattered Pillars*. The strands that bear the greatest emotional freight are that of Temur and Samarkar, and that of Hong-la and Tsering-la, wizards of Tsarepheth, upon whose shoulders falls the responsibility for finding a cure for the plague that has been devastating the city. Surgeons, scientists, wizards: at odds with the ruler of Tsarepheth and Rasa over what is necessary. It is not until refugees arrive from the steppe—Ata Ashra, seeking word of her son Temur, and Tsereg Altantseteg, matriarch of Edene's kin—some of whom are also infected, that they begin to make progress. Even then, it may be too late for Rasa's royal house, the rulers of Tsarepheth: Saadet and her twin Shahruz, on al-Sepehr's orders, have woken the volcano known as the Cold Fire that overlooks the city, and civil unrest has mounted to revolution.

But how these narrative strands all fit together, the final picture that they may present, is something that we must wait for the next volume to reveal.

Understated emotional beats and political intrigue join rooftop chases and burning cities. The lung demon plague is horrifying, disgusting, and a marvelously inventive use of a fantasy setting, as are the gradual changes of the world's sky, which reflects the political reality of nations below. The landscape and inhabitants of Erem, too, are vividly fantastical, with beast-headed ghulim and deadly sunlight.

Much as I enjoyed the novel, it's not without its flaws. It is very much a middle book of a trilogy, and has a number of classic middle book snags. Its focus is more diffuse than its predecessor, its characters' growth less obvious. There is much here that feels as though it's setting up for an ultimate payoff in the final volume, rather than paying off emotionally or thematically before the end of this particular book.

And I confess to some little confusion about what's happening with Edene. I suspect I'll have to wait until the end of the final volume of the trilogy, *Steles of the Sky*, before I can be sure I understand what's going on. As will, no doubt, most other readers. There is no way of knowing at present whose side she and her ghulim will ultimately benefit: Temur's, as she claims, or al-Sepehr's—or the older powers of Erem represented by the ring on her hand.

Whether *Shattered Pillars* is a stunning success or merely a qualified one is a judgment that must wait until *Steles of the Sky* provides a conclusion to the story. In the meanwhile, it is a very shiny middle book, and one that's prompted me to reread *Range of Ghosts* again while I wait for the final volume.

Beth Bernobich, *Queen's Hunt:* A River of Souls Novel
Review: *Ideomancer,* September 1, 2012

Queen's Hunt (2012) is the second volume in Bernobich's River of Souls series, after 2010's *Passion Play.* It's fortunate that it's a book which stands fairly well alone, for I come to it *in medias res,* with no prior knowledge of characters or events.

Despite my failure to do my homework, *Queen's Hunt* is an enjoyable read. It opens apparently some months after the events of *Passion Play.* Ilse Zhalina, publicly estranged from her lover, the disgraced but powerful Lord Raul Kosenmark, is dwelling in a garrison fort, Osterling Keep, distant from Tiralien, capital of the kingdom of Veraene. Their estrangement is a ploy to keep them both safer while Ilse searches by magical means for the powerful jewels of Lir, and while Raul attempts to influence politics to prevent war with the kingdom of Károvi, whose king, Leos Dzavek, has lived several hundred years already. They must tread carefully, because of the enmity of Markus Khandarr, councilor to the king of Veraene. And because Dzavek already has one of the jewels.

In Tiralien, Gerek Hessler joins Kosenmark's household as a secretary under false pretenses, and comes to realize that the man he suspected of terrible things is not actually arrogant and cruelly indifferent. He comes to play a key role in Kosenmark's plans to preserve Ilse.

In Osterling Keep, Ilse comes face to frightening face with Markus Khandarr and encounters another important player: Valara Baussay, heir to the hidden land of Morennioù. Twice taken prisoner—once by the Károvians, once by the garrison at Osterling Keep—Valara has nonetheless been able to keep possession of the second of the three jewels. When she escapes from the garrison prison, she and Ilse join forces to seek the third jewel.

Evading pursuit, distrusting each other, in the end they must confront Leos Dzavek, for the sake of their homelands—and themselves.

What makes things more interesting still is the ontology of Bernobich's world: the characters remember previous lives, and most of the main characters turn out to have leftover unfinished business with each other from generations, even centuries ago, involving (for the most part) love and betrayal. Blood, love, and rhetoric—to borrow a phrase from Tom Stoppard, it turns out that for our protagonists, blood is compulsory, in all of their lives. (They're all blood, you see.)

The prose is strong, expressive, rising occasionally to under-stated elegance. Bernobich has a good hand with a descriptive turn of phrase and a robust grasp of characterization: for the most part, everyone in this book has reasonable, internally con-sistent motivations for the secrets they keep and the actions they take. With intrigue and machinations and danger around every corner, secrets are understandable. The rare moments of trust are startling by comparison.

Queen's Hunt's pace is measured. Far from breakneck, it nonetheless maintains its tension well. Much of this tension is interior, focused on emotions, possibilities, losses and risks: but there is also plenty of physical danger and derring-do. It is a quieter, more personally focused novel than many second-world fantasies. Not only did I enjoy it, but I also found myself finish-ing it in one sitting.

It's a good, solid, agreeable read. I recommend it.

Beth Bernobich, *Allegiance*

Review: *Ideomancer*, September 1, 2013

Allegiance (2013) is Beth Bernobich's fourth novel, and the third in her epic fantasy River of Souls series. It marks the culmination of an arc begun in *Passion Play* (2010) and continued in *Queen's Hunt* (2012), the story of Ilse Zhalina and Lord Raul Kosenmark, and how their fates are entangled with each other and with their homeland, Veraene.

King Leos Dzavek of Károví, whose magic extended his lifespan by centuries, has finally died. Ilse Zhalina and Valara Baussay, the queen of distant Morennioù whom Dzavek's right-hand man Duke Miro Karasek had carried off from her island kingdom, witnessed his death. They witnessed, too, Lir's jewels—magical gems—merge into one single creature, perhaps a god, and disappear into the magical realm of Anderswar. The way is clear for Valara and Ilse to return to their respective homes.

Provided they can escape hostile Károví.

In a surprising move, it is Duke Karasek who offers them his aid...ostensibly without ulterior motive.

While Ilse struggles to cross inhospitable countryside, bearing letters that hold out hope for a lasting peace, back in Veraene her lover Raul Kosenmark is choosing to stop working in the shadows and confront his king directly. Spurred by duty and honor, he will try every last stratagem in his power to prevent a costly and pointless war. But the king of Veraene is a selfish man who brooks no defiance, and Kosenmark's open stand against war will see him imprisoned on charges of treason, awaiting execution. Only Ilse can testify to his innocence, but she doesn't even know the extent of his peril. If she arrives in time, she and Kosenmark must outfox not only the king, but also his closest councilor, the dangerously powerful mage Markus Khandarr, who has grown unpredictably mad.

Allegiance is an odd book. This is not to say it is a bad book: Bernobich's skill with character and with the turn of a phrase have, if anything, improved. But it is *structurally* odd. Two of the things it's doing are diametrically opposed: it is bringing to a culmination the narrative arc of Raul Kosenmark and Ilse Zhalina and the politics of Veraene with which we as readers have been primarily concerned to date. At the same time, it's widening the scope of their world and increasing the number of point-of-view characters, laying the groundwork for future storylines focused on Valara Baussay, among other possibilities. These conflicting narrative impulses—the first, centripetal; the second, centrifugal—combine to create a sense that *Allegiance* is a novel without a center, or rather, with more than one. This impression is compounded by the denouement, a leisurely, meditative, post-triumphal conclusion that leaves *Allegiance*'s loose ends tied off in an unbalanced fashion.

These criticisms may leave you with the notion that I didn't like *Allegiance*. Perish the thought! It may be an interesting failure, but it strives to do fresh, interesting things with the genre. Its failings come from a surfeit of ambition, rather than ambition's lack.

I've said before that an interesting failure is often more entertaining than a novel that's technically successful but has no *heart*. *Allegiance* has heart by the bucketloads. I enjoyed it thoroughly and look forward to reading more of Bernobich's work in the years to come.

Part 4.
And Yet—God Guide Them—Young

Discussions of books by Karen Healey, Amalie Howard, Michelle Sagara, Tamora Pierce, Gwenda Bond, Cassandra Rose Clarke, and Rae Carson

How Stories Shape Worlds:
Guardian of the Dead by Karen Healey

Review: Tor.com, August 5, 2011

Guardian of the Dead (2010) is the YA debut novel of Antipodean author Karen Healey. Published in hardback last year, it made it onto the 2011 finalist panel for the American Library Association's William C. Morris Debut Award. It's just been released in paperback—which is fortunate for those of us who find our discretionary spending rather limited these days, because Guardian is a good book. Despite the fact that the paperback's back copy, with its talk of unhealthy fascinations and shocking revelations and lusts, makes it sound more like tabloid fodder than intelligent and character-driven YA.

Ellie Spencer is seventeen years old and spending her last year of school at boarding school in Christchurch, New Zealand, while her parents celebrate her mother's having survived a bout with cancer by taking a lengthy round-the-world trip. Her life is perfectly normal, from beer cans in the bottom drawer to concerns over friends, exams, and class.

That is, until a bizarre woman with pupil-less eyes and an allergy to the smell of cooked food starts taking far too close an interest in her best friend Kevin, and repeated encounters with school loner Mark Nolan begin to convince her that something is very wrong. As Ellie's eyes are opened to a world of magic and Maori mythology, she learns both that Kevin is in danger from a New Zealand fairy—a patupaiarehe—who wants to steal him away in order to have his children, and that the recent Eyeslasher murders on New Zealand's North Island aren't merely the work of a serial killer with an eye fetish, but represent a danger that threatens everything she holds dear.

Both friendship and betrayal have a part to play in the final confrontation for the fate of New Zealand, but in the end it comes down to Ellie's stubbornness and bravery, her willingness to stand in front of Hine-nui-te-po, the Maori guardian of the dead, and—most of all—her choices.

There's a lot to like in *Guardian of the Dead*. For me, the world of Ellie's New Zealand boarding school resonates with much more familiarity than the high schools of most American young adult fiction—I come from a background where uniforms and examinations are the rule, not the exception—so I imagine it might be a touch unusual for US readers.

The school is merely a backdrop, however. Ellie is a strongly drawn character, recognizably a young adult with the strengths and weaknesses of a seventeen-year-old: her self-consciousness, her body-image worries, her slightly rusty black belt in tae kwon do, her awkwardness in making friends, and her crush on Mark Nolan. The other characters are likewise strongly drawn: Nolan, who thinks of himself as a monster; Kevin, asexual, loyal, abashed; Iris Tsang and the mysterious Reka.

Strong as the characters (some of whom are themselves Maori) might be, the depiction of Maori mythology is even stronger. It makes and shapes the book, a rich layering of history and mythic implication that draws you in and makes you care. As a stranger to this particular mythology, I found it both moving and gripping.

Healey also uses Shakespearean and classical references to good effect. It seems clear to me that this is a story very much concerned with stories themselves and with how stories shape our worlds.

That's not to say that this is a perfect book. The beginning is somewhat slow to get going, and when the focus changes from the more personal story to the wider threat, it feels a little jarring. But despite these small flaws, *Guardian of the Dead* is well-written and compelling. I enjoyed it immensely, and I have no hesitation about recommending it to adult and young adult readers alike.

The Girl Who Died: Karen Healey's *When We Wake*
Review: Tor.com, February 21, 2013

When We Wake (2013) is New Zealand author Karen Healey's third novel, after *Guardian of the Dead* (2010) and *The Shattering* (2011). It's an excellent YA novel. It's also really excellent science fiction: I stayed awake far later than I would otherwise have done to finish it.

In 2027, sixteen-year-old Tegan Oglietti dies. A hundred years in the future, her cryonically preserved body is revived by the Australian military—the first successful cryonic revival. The Girl Who Died is an instant celebrity and the government's favorite guinea pig. All she wants to do is grieve her old life and try to build some semblance of a "normal" new one, but with her footsteps dogged by the media, a fundamentalist sect who believes she should commit suicide, and a minor case of futureshock, it's not that easy. But Tegan's stubborn. She goes to school, she makes friends. Bethari, the army-brat young journalist. Joph, the brilliant chemistry student walking around in a haze of her own creations. Abdi, the talented musician from Somalia who's almost as much an outsider as Tegan is in immigrant-hostile 22nd-century Australia.

But the military hasn't told Tegan the truth about why they chose to revive her. When she begins to discover the secrets they've been keeping from her.... Well, it turns out that military secrets have horrifying consequences, and not just for Tegan herself.

This is, by me, a really good book. It works on several levels of engagement: I'm trying, still, to disentangle the things that I admire about it *now*, as a work of literature that appeals to me as an adult, from the things that should make it work for its target audience. I think it comes down to voice. Healey really *nails* voice. Not only her own authorial voice, which we've seen before in her other work, but the voice of *When We Wake*'s protagonist, Tegan. It's distinctive, and compelling, and also has a sly, retrospective *I'm-not-telling-you-everything-at-once* quality, a hinted frame narrative, the reasons for which we discover in the conclusion.

The adolescent friendships, relationships, embarrassments, and concerns, come across as spot on. Tegan's friendship with Bethari, and how Bethari's finding her sexually attractive as well, plays out realistically. It's only a moment in the narrative: but it's the kind of natural, queer-friendly moment that a whole lot of novels might either elide entirely or blow up into a Big Teachable Point. (Perhaps my experience in this regard is slightly out-of-date, but one goes with what one knows.)

There's also a lot of pointed social critique in *When We Wake*. Healey's future Australia isn't a dystopia: in terms of gendered and religious tolerance and environmental consciousness, it's portrayed as explicitly *better* than Tegan's original time. But thanks to climate change, a lot of quiet resource struggle is going on in the background, and in part thanks to this, anti-immigrant sentiment has reached a vicious peak. No one receives resident visas to the future Australia anymore, only temporary or student ones. Illegal immigrants who reach Australia are kept in detention camps, about which the media doesn't report. This affects—strains—Tegan's friendship with Abdi.

Social tensions about resources, the status of unrecognized immigrant persons, and survival in the face of climate change all come together in the climax of Tegan's story.

I have a handful of minor criticisms. The emotional freight of some of the interactions between Tegan and her friends on occasion comes across as a little heavy-handed, and the climax, for me, happens a little too quickly. But on the whole? This is a very good book.

A sequel, *While We Run*, is expected,[1] but *When We Wake* stands on its own.

---

1 *While We Run* was published in 2014. It's a sequel from Abdi's point of view.

Almost a Book: *The Almost Girl* by Amalie Howard
Review: Tor.com, January 6, 2014

The older I get, the harder I am to satisfy. Certainly I grow crankier: Amalie Howard's *The Almost Girl* (2014) impressed me with how thoroughly it managed to annoy me. And not, I hasten to add, for the most common reasons: retrograde or thoughtless prejudices, poor treatment of its female characters, poor or clichéd prose.

No, *The Almost Girl* annoyed me because it is *almost* more than a set of shiny ideas thrown together with no particular concern for worldbuilding, pace, character development, and logic. It is, in fact, *almost* a book.

The Almost Girl is a Young Adult novel. It's not always just to judge Young Adult novels by the same criteria we apply to works for an older audience, just as it's not always fair to judge tragedy by the same criteria as comedy: they have different goals and purposes, and speak to different experiences of life. A good deal of discussion of YA as a category stumbles when it comes to making this distinction: the heightened emotionality, the fraught intensity of close relationships, love and treachery, life and death—in short, the qualities that appear to many an adult critic as overdone angst—reflects the ardent fervor of adolescent inner life.[2]

But it's possible to take that emotional intensity too far—to add to it, or to create it from, so many disparate elements that it breaks the suspension of disbelief and invites bewilderment. You can have a murderous mad-scientist father and a dying liege lord and an upbringing scarred by a violent world and a sister you're afraid you might have to kill, but it seems rather excessive thereafter to add long-lost anti-establishment mothers, triple help-

---

2 I remember being fifteen. Everything important to me felt like a matter of life and death.

ings of treachery and deceit, and falling in love with someone you intend to betray.

Then again, I'm not fifteen anymore, and quite possibly I'd have had a great deal more tolerance for the combination of these elements if *The Almost Girl* had not, in addition, combined portal fantasy with technological dystopia. Two great tastes, I grant you; but I'm far from convinced they taste great together.

Riven, our protagonist, comes from a parallel world to Earth. A world in many senses both post-apocalyptic and dystopian: ravaged by terrible wars, her home has developed into a repressive authoritarian technological dictatorship. By the age of fourteen, she was an accomplished killer and a general in service to her prince. At the age of *seventeen*, she's spent three years bouncing between American high schools in search of her prince's long-lost "brother" Caden, who was spirited away to our Earth shortly after his birth. When she finally finds him, her task is to bring him home regardless of his wishes: to a home where his likely fate is death. A task complicated by the fact that she's hardly the only person searching for Caden: there's a dastardly royal uncle and the aforementioned murderous mad-scientist father in the mix, as well.

The juxtaposition of other-world technological dystopia and modern American high school brings a number of the novel's… inconsistencies…to light. Riven is surprisingly *au fait* with some aspects of popular culture (including *The Princess Diaries*) but is remarkably lax about her cover story, to the point where she says, when introducing herself, "Where I come from, we don't have two names, only one." Presumably in order to enroll in high school, or operate her motorbike, or rent a motel room, she has to have some kind of documentation that wouldn't raise too many American eyebrows? Documentation, one presumes, that has a dominant-culture form of name to avoid attracting too much attention?

A girl can only handwave so many things before the effort all gets too much. Like the number of coincidences that contribute to the progress of the plot. Like the fact that so much Cool Shit, so many disparate elements, get introduced with insufficient development, until it begins to feel as though the author poured Cool Shit into a blender, but the blender wasn't quite working properly, there was a thin layer of grit in the bottom, and chocolate went in with the beetroot and onions.

I may have over-extended my metaphor, there. But if I were to list *all* the things that niggled at my potential enjoyment, we'd be here until tomorrow. After the dozenth time some new curveball—emotional or worldbuilding/plot-related—flew in with little-to-no incluing ahead of time, in fact, I stopped keeping track.

That said, Howard's prose is brisk and straightforward, and the immediacy of the first-person-present-tense plays to its strengths. And in many ways, the novel's overall emotional tenor, if not its events, reminds me of Sarah J. Maas's *Throne of Glass* (2012)—not a book I can personally recommend, but one which many people seem to have enjoyed[3]—so I feel confident that Howard will find her audience.

Alas, I also feel confident that I cavil too much about *details* to be among it.

3 By my lights, at least, Howard is a much better writer than Maas.

Ghosts and Friendship: *Touch* by Michelle Sagara
Review: Tor.com, January 13, 2014

Touch (2014) is a novel I've been looking forward to for some time. *Silence* (2012), its well-received predecessor, was Michelle Sagara's first foray into Young Adult waters: a story of ghosts and friendship, grief and compassion, and higher stakes than are initially apparent. As a sequel, *Touch* more than lives up to expectations.

It can be difficult to review quiet books. Books where the emphasis is on the interpersonal moments, where all the freight falls onto the relationships between characters, on subtle cues and moments. Books where the tension is mostly between people of good will and the exigencies of circumstance. *Touch* isn't a flashy book. You only realize how well it's succeeded as a novel when you pause to reflect on how *much* it's made you care, and in what ways.

That is not to say that there's no action and no derring-do. There is. Just, like *Silence*, it's not exactly the point.

In *Silence*, teenage Emma Hall, recently bereaved of her boyfriend Nathan, discovered that she could see ghosts and affect the world of the dead. Emma is a necromancer, a potentially very powerful necromancer, and the vast majority of necromancers are deeply unpleasant people, led by the Queen of the Dead. But Emma and her friends Allison, Amy, and Michael—and the mysterious duo Chase and Eric, who've trained to fight necromancers—are decent sorts. Emma, in fact, is the kind of person who will put herself in danger to rescue a dead child from suffering as a ghost, but her power means she's a target for other necromancers, who want to use her.

In *Touch*, more of the narrative is carried by Emma's best friend Allison. Allison has no special powers or training, and

Chase—who distrusts all necromancers, and has grown fond of Allison—wants her to stay away from the great big shiny target that Emma's become. But Allison isn't the kind of person who walks away from her friends. Even if it threatens to put her life at risk.

Emma, on the other hand, has been reunited with Nathan—in a manner of speaking; Nathan is still dead, but his ghost has returned home, far sooner than anyone thought possible for a ghost to do. This is a complicated situation for both of them, and meanwhile, Emma's mother has brought home a new boyfriend/potential partner to introduce to her. Necromancers still threaten her life, and the lives of her friends, and Emma has begun to wrestle with the question of whether it's *right* to put the people in her life in danger just by being around them.

Readers of Michelle Sagara under her other name, Michelle West, will be familiar with the mood of creeping dread, the undertone of horror, which *Touch* at times evokes. For all that this is a novel deeply concerned with loyalty, with healthy friendships, and with human decency, it doesn't hesitate to wrap cold fingers around your spine and yank when the moment calls for it. Sagara's characters are believable, flawed, and very human, and make for compelling reading.

Reflecting on *Touch*, in some ways I'm put in mind of *Buffy The Vampire Slayer* in the early years. Not the humor, not the apocalypses, not the world—but the way in which a group of friends come together to support each other in the face of painful events and weird shit. I really enjoyed it, and I look forward to seeing how Sagara resolves the dilemma confronting her characters in *Touch*'s final pages. More like this, please.

Tell No One Where You're Bound—
Tamora Pierce's *Mastiff*

Review: Tor.com, December 6, 2011

Mastiff (2011) is the highly anticipated third and final installment of Tamora Pierce's Beka Cooper novels, after 2006's *Terrier* and 2009's *Bloodhound*. Three years have passed since the events of *Bloodhound*. Beka is still partnered with Tunstall and still assigned as a Dog in the Lower City, where she has quite a reputation for hunting criminals, both in her own right and as the handler of the scent hound Achoo. The night after she buries her fiancé, the Lord Provost himself arrives on her doorstep with secret orders: dress and pack in haste.

Beka and Tunstall, together with the Lord Provost's most trusted mage, an odd duck called Farmer Cape, are summoned to the Summer Palace. Four-year-old Prince Gareth has been abducted by people who don't hesitate to slaughter everyone in their way. The magic used suggests that this is a plot that reaches the highest echelons of the kingdom. Great mages and powerful nobles alike are annoyed by King Roger's plans for taxation, and as Beka and her companions come to learn, the prince's health has been magically linked to his parents'. His suffering is their suffering; his death, should he die, their death.

Joined by Lady Sabine of Macayhill, a lady knight and Tunstall's lover, Beka and her companions set out in pursuit of the prince, a long, difficult hunt, with dangers at every turn. Young Gareth has been disguised as a slave and taken north in a slave caravan.

Beka and company are already days behind. More than once, they miss their quarry by mere hours. When they finally do catch up, it is to walk into a trap. One of their party is a traitor, and it is up to Beka to escape the trap and rescue the prince.

Mastiff is, I think, perhaps the darkest and most mature—in theme, if not in content—of Pierce's books to date. Emotionally, it hits a lot of less than shiny and happy notes: Beka's complicated feelings toward her dead fiancé, Holborn, wind about the narrative. It's a very accurate picture of someone who's fallen out of love—and feels guilty about the jerk they fell out of love with. The kidnapping of a child, too, is not a cheery event, and nor are the deaths Beka comes across in pursuit. Nor, either, the treatment of slaves.

Which isn't to say it's a book full of doom and gloom. It's well-paced and well-characterized, and Beka is possessed of a sense of humor, although the conceit that this is her account written down in her journal is a little hard to believe. All the characters, including newcomers Farmer Cape, the mage, and the lady knight Sabine are fascinating (and in case you're wondering, yes, I would read a whole book about Sabine of Macayhill: I'm biased toward people who start—and win—tavern brawls) and the foursome, or rather sextet (counting the semi-divine cat Pounce and the scent hound Achoo), have an interesting dynamic on the road north. The interlude at the castle of Queensgrace is particularly well done, I thought: but then I have a soft spot for capers and "do they know that we know that they know that we know" types of maneuvering.

The truth of betrayal turns out to be heart-wrenching. It's to Pierce's credit that she makes it believably in character, as well.

Mastiff is an excellent read. It's gripping from the very first pages, and it builds steam all the way to a compelling conclusion. With, of course, moments of humor and touching emotion along the way. I recommend it wholeheartedly: it's not just a good YA fantasy, but a fine book in its own right.

Marked with the Serpent as Agents of Betrayal: *Blackwood* by Gwenda Bond

Review: Tor.com, September 3, 2012

Published by Strange Chemistry, the fledgling YA imprint of Angry Robot Books, *Blackwood* (2012) is Gwenda Bond's debut novel. If this is the quality of Strange Chemistry's novels going forward, I'd say they're set to be a success: as a debut, *Blackwood* isn't half bad.

In the late 16th century, 114 people disappeared from the island of Roanoke. The "Lost Colony" has passed into historical myth and mystery, a story for the tourists. But when one hundred and fourteen people go missing overnight on modern Roanoke Island, it seems the old mystery may be closer than anyone realized. Seventeen-year-old Miranda Blackwood, misfit daughter of the town drunk, and Phillips Rawling, the juvenile delinquent son of the town's police chief who hears ghosts, find themselves at the center of the new mystery. Eluding federal agents and long-dead alchemists, their only hope is to uncover their relationship to the historical Lost Colony in time to save today's Missing Persons—not only the missing, but the whole island; not only the island, but *maybe* the world.

Blackwood offers plenty to like. The prose is breezy and witty by turns, with a definite authorial voice. It carries you along, unobtrusive without being bland, maintaining a pacey, urgent tension from the moment the missing persons are revealed to be *missing*. Miranda Blackwood's conflicted relationship with her father is real and human, rather than cliché. Very early on in the course of events, she learns he's been murdered, and her reaction combines relief and heartbreak: she loved him, but now she doesn't have to take care of him anymore.

She's also a geek who swears with *frak*, about which I alternated between finding overdone and annoying, and validating for my girlish admiration of all things early-season BSG.

Phillips Rawling is likewise interesting; prankster and car thief, his father calls him home from school because Police Chief Rawlings hopes that his son's predilection for hearing ghosts might help solve the disappearances. Once back on the island, though, Phillips makes straight for Miranda, convinced she's in danger. His authority-defying ways make it hard for his parents to protect him—and they do try, especially when it starts to look like the forces of history are pushing Miranda and Phillips onto opposite sides.

About those forces of history....

It turns out that John Dee, the famous 16th-century astrologer, hatched a plot to pack the original Roanoke colony with alchemists, who were to create an instrument that could make Dee and his followers immortal. This didn't come off so well the first time around, but now possessing the body of Miranda's dead father, and with acolytes to assist him, Dee means to complete his great work and acquire both immortality and earthly power.

It is here that *Blackwood* stumbles. A brisk, breezy read on first glance, the plot involving John Dee is convoluted and full of lacunae that don't stand up to closer examination. While I confess I'm fiercely picky when I come across the alchemist/astrologer/mathematician in fiction, and while Dee was an ardent proponent of British expansionism, the chronology of his life mandates against any but the most cursory of involvements in the Roanoke expeditions. The founding of the original Roanoke colonies and their destruction/disappearance took place between 1584 and 1590: from 1583 to 1589, John Dee and Edward Kelley were traveling on the continent, enjoying the patronage of aristocrats in Poland and the Holy Roman Empire. (Dee was shopping for a more interested patron than Elizabeth I, but by 1587, Kelley had begun to eclipse his former mentor. Dee eventually returned to England without him, finding that his library had been ransacked by a mob in his absence. He was to die in poverty sometime during the winter of 1608/9.) And Dee's well-attested Christian piety (although it took some odd forms, and his dream of reunifying Protestant and Catholic theologies was doomed from the outset), makes him, to my mind at least, a strange fit for the role of murderous devil.

Leaving aside matters of chronology, the sad fact is that Dee's plot makes little sense. The outlines of it also bear little relationship to alchemy as it was practiced during the 16th century, but that may be beside the point. Functionally, he's a modern-day Dark Lord: his scheme doesn't have to make sense; it's just there to provide a threat that drives our protagonists to act. But when our protagonists, Miranda and Phillips, come face to face with the resurrected John Dee, *Blackwood*'s pace starts to stagger. The final third of the novel is noticeably uneven, and the conclusion is made of rather less awesome than I was hoping for.

But I'm judging *Blackwood* against the highest standards of the field. First-novel teething trouble aside—which I beg leave to doubt any fourteen-year-old will much notice—it's a brisk, entertaining read. *Blackwood* is a promising debut: I look forward to seeing what Gwenda Bond does next.

Pirates, Assassins, and Magic:
Cassandra Rose Clarke's *The Assassin's Curse*

Review: Tor.com, October 22, 2012

Kirkus Book Reviews, home of famously cranky and hard-to-please reviewers, unbent so far as to give *The Assassin's Curse* (2012) a starred review. With praise and blurbing from the likes of Tamora Pierce and Adrian Tchaikovsky, I doubt my sour opinion will lose Clarke's publishers much sleep. But the fact remains: I can't join in the paeans of praise.

I guess this makes me even crankier than *Kirkus*, because when it comes to *The Assassin's Curse*, I find myself distinctly under-impressed. Which is at least a little odd, because on the face of it, Clarke's debut novel has a number of elements that, going on past experience, should have hit my bulletproof kink buttons. Pirates! Assassins! Enemies thrown together by circumstance and forced to work together!

Ananna is a daughter of pirates who has always wanted to captain her own ship. Instead, her parents decide to marry her off to the handsome yet inexperienced son of a wealthy allied pirate clan. Rather than accept her arranged marriage, Ananna steals a camel and makes a break for freedom. In the markets of Lisirra, she encounters a mysterious grey-eyed woman who knows more than she should, and a young assassin with a scarred face—sent by her intended husband's family to avenge the slight against their honor. When she accidentally saves the assassin's life, she fulfills the conditions of a curse that binds him to protect her on pain of pain. Pursued by magical beings from the Otherword, or the "Mist," they set out together to find some way of releasing the assassin, whose name is Naji, from his curse. First they have to travel across the desert to a witch whom Naji used to know well and whom he still loves, and then by sea to the north, to the

Isles of the Sky, where just possibly there is someone who knows how to undo an impossible curse.

Alas, *The Assassin's Curse* has a number of niggling flaws that undermine its initially appealing picture. Not least among which is the typical debut novel trick of trying to stretch a half-pound of plot to fill a full pound-size container: *The Assassin's Curse* fails to sufficiently connect its incidents in such a way as to consistently maintain pace and tension. There's a lot of traveling, a lot of movement—but often it seems this sound and fury signifies… well, not much. Moments of peril resolve themselves without *accumulating*, and as a result emotional impact is lost.

Speaking of emotional impact, or at least emotional connection: I don't feel it with Clarke's first-person protagonist, Ananna. The idiomatic, naturalistic style shows great promise—Clarke's technical abilities with prose are nothing to sneeze at for a debut novelist, with some strong turns of phrase and a nice, if perhaps over-liberal, touch with description—but Ananna's wants and fears all seem shallow. You'd think someone who'd just left their parents and their whole life behind would have a few second thoughts, but Ananna's inner life reflects an unthinking self-absorption that nags at me like an unscratched itch.

And, too, there is a small unexplained logical flaw: why does Ananna so readily accept the need to free Naji of his curse? Isn't it useful to have an assassin forced to protect you—and might he not be in a position to kill you again, as soon as he's released? Perhaps her brain's clouded by finding him attractive, a development that I could not help but find painfully predictable.

I'd like to be able to cut *The Assassin's Curse* some slack for the conventions of its genre and the expectations of its audience, but the plain truth is, it rubs me entirely the wrong way. It is a book not without technical accomplishments, and a pirate/assassin pairing has at least the benefit of somewhat more novelty than werewolf/vampire. But the strongest emotion I can muster in its regard is a sort of lukewarm goodwill.

It's not a *bad* book, exactly. But it most assuredly failed to work for me.

The Girl of Fire and Thorns and *The Crown of Embers,* or the Immensely Readable Novels of Rae Carson

Column: Tor.com, September 26, 2012

The Girl of Fire and Thorns (2011), Rae Carson's first novel, made its debut this time last year. Immensely readable, and original in its execution, it's no surprise that it immediately began to garner plaudits and acclaim.

Here be spoilers for *The Girl of Fire and Thorns,* and mild spoilerishness for its sequel, *The Crown of Embers* (2012).

Elisa is an unusual heroine: she bears a Godstone in her navel, a sign that she's marked out by divinity for a special destiny—or perhaps a special sacrifice. But she's also the younger, fatter, plainer of two princesses, married off to the weak king of a desert nation, a king who has chosen to keep their marriage secret. Elisa's new kingdom is in turmoil, threatened by Invierne invaders who have powerful magic. Kidnapped from her husband's palace by revolutionaries from the north, Elisa has to grow into her destiny. When the novel ends, she's a ruling queen, having defeated her enemies and lost her husband—not to mention the man who could have been her lover.

Carson's approach to her epic fantasy (marketed as Young Adult, but dear epic fantasy readers, do not *dare* overlook it on those grounds) is marked by solid, interesting worldbuilding, with an intriguing strain of piety. A deity active in the world yet inexplicable and rather hands-off when it comes to *useful* interventions: that brings back memories of my long-gone childhood Catholicism, which always has the chance of being really irritating. But Carson integrates her theology well into her world and the life of her protagonist, avoiding any number of potential pitfalls with the same deftness that she employs as she sets up and then *proceeds to subvert* the by-now all-too-typical romantic love triangle.

It's this mindful, playful subversion of several common tropes that elevates *The Girl of Fire and Thorns* from a well-executed fantasy with a vivid and immediate voice[4] into something delightful[5] and refreshing.

And it's the element of subversion that *The Crown of Embers* lacks, making Carson's second novel less successful, on the whole, than her first.

This is far less severe a criticism than it would be for a novel whose author *hadn't* made her debut with one of the most successful[6] self-contained epic fantasies I'd read in years. *The Crown of Embers* is immensely readable: I inhaled it in one sitting, racing to the finish in less than three hours. There is intrigue and death and travel, assassins and assassination attempts, and a royal council largely determined to either marry their interloping reigning queen off or otherwise cripple her influence…and the Invierne are back. They want Elisa, and the Godstone she bears. Alive, if possible—but dead will do.

Elisa sets out on a quest to outwit her enemies, both foreign and domestic, and find the "gate of life" named in the scriptures, in the hopes that its power will be sufficient to bolster her authority vis-à-vis her scheming royal councilors and to defend her kingdom from the sorcerers of the Invierne, whose armies devastated the outskirts of her capital during the events of *The Girl of Fire and Thorns*. The traditional arc of the fantasy quest-plot here is well-executed, with driving tension and sympathetic charac-

4   First-person, present-tense, from Elisa's point of view.

5   Delightful in the sense that certain developments delighted me on the grounds that Carson was doing something *interesting*. The novel doesn't necessarily have a delightful mood, being in parts rather on the grim and tense side.

6   In the technical sense, although I understand it was also well-received in the marketplace.

terization of all Elisa's traveling companions—and an excellent twist in the tail, when it comes to climax and denouement.

But alongside the quest, *The Crown of Embers* is invested in developing the romantic tension between Elisa and the commander of her personal guard, Hector. While Carson does a solid job working through the complications that could inhibit the growth of an egalitarian partnership between a monarch and her liegeman, Elisa's unwillingness to speak her feelings aloud—and the resulting will-she won't-she *no she still won't* unfulfilled sexual tension—acts as a dragging sea anchor on more realized and interesting character development. The fact that neither party actually *used their words* (or even, it seemed, seriously considered using them) to have a serious discussion of what they mean to each other and how the exigencies of their respective positions do or should affect their conduct proved, in my view, something of an annoying flaw, particularly as Carson had previously established her credentials when it came to subverting standard tropes.

The Girl of Fire and Thorns is a self-contained volume. *The Crown of Embers* concludes with a cliffhanger. They're both immensely entertaining and very readable. My minor irritations with *Embers'* romance plot aside, this is good fantasy, and I'm really looking forward to seeing what happens next.

I Think We Just Saw History Being Made:
Rae Carson's *The Bitter Kingdom*

Review: Tor.com, August 27, 2013

The Bitter Kingdom (2013) is the final volume in Rae Carson's debut trilogy, after 2011's *The Girl of Fire and Thorns* and last year's *The Crown of Embers*. These novels may be marketed at the YA audience, but adult epic fantasy aficionados will also find them worth their while: Carson knows how to tell a damn good story.

The Bitter Kingdom starts hard on the heels of the events of *The Crown of Embers*. Elisa, queen of Joya d'Arena and bearer of a magic "Godstone" in her navel, faces fresh challenges to her rule. Her kingdom is threatened by civil war, as one of her noblemen, the Conde Eduardo, together with one of her generals, has risen in revolt and seized her capital. The commander of her royal guard, Hector—a man whom she loves and whom she intends to marry in order to make a political alliance with his powerful family—has been captured by the Joyans' longtime enemies, the nation of Invierne. Elisa means first to ride to his rescue, second to compel the Invierno to accept a peace, and third to put down the revolt against her rule back home in Joya d'Arena.

In that order.

"We run."

The opening line of *The Bitter Kingdom* sets the pace for the pages that follow. The first-person present-tense narrative lends itself well to breathless, breakneck, headlong intensity: it grabs you by the throat from the offing, and doesn't let go.

> "My companions—an assassin, a lady-in-waiting, and
> a failed sorcerer—are all more accustomed than I am
> to hard travel, and I dare not slow us down."
> (Carson, 2013, 1)

Elisa and her small band of companions race across the land-scape in the best traditions of heroic fantasy. Belén, Mara, and the Invierno failed sorcerer Storm are joined first by a half-Joyan half-Invierno child called Mula and after the daring rescue, by Hector. In Umbra de Deus, overshadowed by two volcanoes, Elisa and her company encounter Storm's family and two members of the Invierno ruling council, the Deciregi. Magic, betrayal, conspiracies, *more* daring rescues and dreadful revelations combine explosively.

And this is only *The Bitter Kingdom*'s midpoint.

It's inevitable that the second half of the book should suffer by comparison. Materials can only be maintained under tension for so long before they undergo ill effects, and this is as true for narratives as for physical substances. There's only so much head-long racing a body can read....

It's to Carson's credit, however, that the latter half of the book only suffers a *little*. Elisa and her brave band race the invading Invierno Deciregi to the city of Basanjuan, where she means to meet her fellow queens, her sister Alodia and her friend Cos-mé, and form an alliance. (Through snowy mountains and deep mines filled with poisonous scorpions: the nod to Tolkien made *this* reviewer, at least, smile.)

Elisa's triumph is completed when she regains her capital and her crown. Along the way, she has lost her Godstone, having carried out the task divinely ordained for her to perform. That task had nothing to do with the political struggles she's faced. As Hector says, "Your Godstone didn't drive you to do all those things. You did them all *yourself*" (Carson, 2013, 368).

The Bitter Kingdom marks the culmination of one of the more interesting takes on the "Chosen One" *topos* in fantasy I've yet read. Unlike gritty, so-called "grimdark," fantasy, which subverts the idea of the "Chosen One" in a wholly different way, Carson has subverted the idea of the "Chosen One" with gentle irony. Elisa is *Chosen* for a task that makes sense only in the "mind of God," as the novel has it. It is her *own* choices that catapult her to *political* pre-eminence. Being queen and the savior of her country is all on her, not on fate.

And that, combined with Carson's lean, driven storytelling style, is why I'll be recommending this trilogy far and wide. I may quibble with some of the narrative choices, such as the decision to include chapters from Hector's point of view only while he and Elisa are separated. But on the whole?

On the whole, *The Bitter Kingdom*—and indeed the entire trilogy—is an achievement of which Carson can be rightly proud. Read it. It's more than worth your time.

Part 5.
Playing Female — Or Not

Mass Effect, Tomb Raider, and *Dishonored*

Mass Effect and the Normalization of the Woman Hero

Sleeps With Monsters: Tor.com, May 29, 2012

Let's get something out of the way before we start. The *Mass Effect* franchise ending? IT DOES NOT EXIST, AND WE SHALL NEVER SPEAK OF IT AGAIN. Somewhere in an alternate universe, Garrus and Tali are having cocktails on a beach, while Jack teaches junior biotics how to swear, is all I'm saying.[1]

But that's not what I want to talk about today. What I want to talk about is how—provided one plays as Commander Jane rather than Commander John—the *Mass Effect* series normalizes the idea of the Woman Hero.

You may have noticed that Woman Hero is my term of choice here, rather than Heroine. Whether we like it or not, *heroine* is still a word that embodies connotations that differ in many and manifest ways from *hero*. Gothic and romance novels have heroines. Thrillers and action stories have heroes: if these also have *heroines*, the heroine almost always takes second stage to the *hero*. Where the *heroine* has pride of place, she's (again, almost always) intimately connected to, or in some way (emotionally, intellectually, or politically) dependent upon, a *hero*, whose actions and reactions are either vital to her as a character, or to the resolution of plot and theme. The reverse is much less true, and much less *often* true (once one might have said *Not at all true*), when the Hero stands center stage. The Hero does not depend: his actions are not *contingent* actions.

1 Other people like Chuck Wendig (http://terribleminds.com/ramble/2012/03/28/mass-effect-the-story-is-the-game/) and Brit Mandelo (http://britmandelo.livejournal.com/735348.html) have had things to say about Bioware's failure to stick the dismount of an otherwise brilliantly written RPG series. So let's leave it there.

Heroine is a word with a history. That history carries with it a metric crapton(ne) of implications, a bunch of which place *heroine* in opposition or in contrast to *hero*.

Commander Jane Shepard is not merely our protagonist and player-avatar in the *Mass Effect* franchise. She's an ἥρως[2] in practically the original Greek sense: a warrior of outstanding (legendary, potentially superhuman) achievements. Moreover, since Shepard's interactions with other characters remain substantially the same regardless of whether one is a John or a Jane, it's established that Commander Jane Shepard isn't remarkable because she's a woman. She's extraordinary because she's *Shepard*. This is reinforced by the ubiquity of other female characters who possess a wide array of competences: Gunnery Chief Ashley Williams, asari archaeologist/information broker Liara T'Soni, quarian engineer Tali'Zorah vas Neema, Doctor Chakwas, Miranda Lawson, the asari Justicar Samara, and human weapon of mass destruction Jack ("Subject Zero"). And although the visible people of the human Alliance's high command trend male, *Mass Effect*'s galaxy at large is populated with a multitude of interesting women, both human and alien.

And Shepard.

Marie Brennan wrote something pertinent to this disquisition at SF Novelists, not so long ago. In "The Effect She Can Have,"[3] concerning another Bioware property, *Dragon Age 2*, Brennan says:

> It took me a while, though, to figure out that there was something else going on in my reaction—something beyond appreciation of the clever structural game the writers were playing.
>
> *She.*

2 http://www.perseus.tufts.edu/hopper/
text?doc=Perseus:text:1999.04.0072:entry=h(/rws.

3 http://www.sfnovelists.com/2012/05/16/the-effect-she-can-have/.

…[I]t allows you to experience the novelty of a woman being the most important damn person *in the world.*

The most important damn person in the world.

There's one scene in particular in *Mass Effect 3* where that's hammered home with a vengeance. How often is the "most famous officer" referred to with a female pronoun? A party member and companion, Dr. Liara T'Soni, says, "Shepard was also a deadly tactical fighter. Most enemies never saw her coming. She was a soldier, and a leader—one who made peace where she could. And it was a privilege to know her."

The dialogue will be different depending on the game one plays. But the sentiment is the same. Commander Jane Shepard isn't an extraordinary *woman.* She's simply extraordinary. Full stop. No qualifiers. When one considers the amount of crap extraordinary people who are also women have directed at them even today—the likes of Hilary Clinton and Angela Merkel in the political realm,[4] household names like Lady Gaga, writers like Toni Morrison—this is immensely validating.[5]

In "The Effect She Can Have," Brennan goes on to mention the dislocating effect of "having people speak in such monumental terms about this woman. About *any* woman…. [A] male character can inspire such loyalty in their followers, or scare a room full of people just by walking in"—but as she notes, the female equivalent of this power fantasy remains a (slightly shocking) novelty.

4   Whatever one thinks of their politics, there's no escaping the fact that achieving their present positions took extraordinary drive.

5   In researching this post, I discovered that Canada's first female Major-General was appointed in 1994, while in 1995, Norway appointed the first ever female commander of a submarine. And as of 2005, the British forces have permitted female soldiers to enter the new Special Reconnaissance Regiment — which is the only Special Forces regiment in Britain to recruit women. Speaking of extraordinary.

Whatever the *Mass Effect* franchise's gender-related world-building flaws (there are male gaze issues with the presentation of the "matriarchal" asari as a species, although these are less pronounced in the final analysis than I feared they would be—and rather less pronounced than many television series that have featured female aliens: I'm looking at *you, Torchwood* and *Doctor Who*—and the presentation of the female krogan in *Mass Effect 3* as more rational and less warlike than the males is not necessarily the *best* of all possible decisions that could be made), the manner in which it assumes (on grounds of gender, at least) an equal-opportunity future (and peoples its background across the three installments with human women and men of all orientations: I confess, I did a little chair-dance when I realized there were romance options in *ME3* that *only* worked for characters attracted to the same sex) is a choice that remains radical in its implications.

The manner in which it presents the Woman Hero as *normal*, as a character, and as a choice, in the case of Commander Jane Shepard, also remains radical. Playing as Commander John Shepard, I found myself annoyed at how predictable the hero's development—and dialogue—could be. Playing as Commander *Jane*....

It was refreshing, and satisfying, and disorienting all at once. But the arc of the *story* is the same. Merely by removing the emphasis from the *Woman* part of *heroine* to the *Hero* part—in creating a *Woman Hero* who is extraordinary as a Hero, rather than as a Woman—Bioware made the experience innovative and fresh.

Perhaps in another generation or three, the Woman Hero will be as Normal (and annoying) as the square-jawed Hero himself. But right now?

Right now, I find Commander Jane Shepard *delightful.*

Tomb Raider is Bloody Awesome

Sleeps With Monsters: Tor.com, June 25, 2013

Following the wee kerfuffle[6],[7] last summer, I'd no plans to play *Tomb Raider*; combine the producer's statements with a vague memory of loathing the franchise ten years ago and a working knowledge of how gaming tends to treat female characters in general, and you understand why I might be reluctant.

Then the game came out. People whose opinions I respect began to say good things about it. I read an interview with Rhianna Pratchett,[8] the lead writer. I found a reasonably priced copy and said to myself, *Well, maybe we should give it a shot.*

The last thing I expected, when I cracked the cover, was to look around sixteen hours later and discover I'd played through the night and most of the next morning, hooked on the narrative, determined to find out what happened next.[9]

As narratives go, *Tomb Raider*'s is fairly straightforward. Survive. Escape. Rescue some mates. (Mostly survive.) Where it excels, though? Tone. Character. The deployment of emotional realism.[10]

6   http://www.themarysue.com/lara-croft-misogyny/.

7   http://kotaku.com/5917400/youll-want-to-protect-the-new-less-curvy-lara-croft.

8   http://www.eurogamer.net/articles/2012-11-01-rewriting-tomb-raider-a-conversation-with-rhianna-pratchett.

9   The last time I lost track of time that thoroughly for that long was with *Dragon Age: Origins*, the December of my final undergrad year. Mind you, DA:O is really more of a thirty-six-hour game than a sixteen-hour one. Or a sixty-hour one, if you're a completist.

10 Not very realistic: the treatment of archaeology and archaeological projects. You need to know where you intend to survey and/or conduct excavation before you set out, because not only is it time- and labor-intensive, but you need paperwork, people. If

The crew of the *Endurance* are searching for the lost (mythical, Japanese) kingdom of Yamatai. Part archaeological expedition, part reality TV show, most of the participants seem to be under the delusion that one can get rich through archaeology if you just find the right site. But a dramatic shipwreck intervenes! Cast ashore on a mysterious island, you finally regain consciousness tied up in a cave full of bones and dead people. Thus begins your adventure as Lara Croft. The tone of things for the first act is set by the words delivered by the voice-over actor: "This," she says, "is going to hurt."

(Other telling phrases delivered with conviction: "What *is* this place?" "You can do this, Lara," and "Oh god, what am I doing?")

Let's be clear about one thing: *Tomb Raider* isn't a fluffy adventure. It starts out with a survival-horror aesthetic and ramps back to merely brutal and bloody.[11] It isn't, however (some elements of art design aside), gratuitously so. Naturally this is a judgment of taste, one based in part upon what I believe the game to be attempting as a piece of art: the material remains open to other interpretations.

So what *is* *Tomb Raider* doing, as art? It makes a damn solid attempt at charting the development of a character from a college

---

you don't have at least the landowner's permission, and in most cases government permission, it's not archaeology, it's theft. Which happens a lot—the global trade in illicit antiquities is worth millions—but it's not in the least respectable. See the 1970 UNESCO Convention on the Means of Prohibiting and Preventing the Illicit Import, Export and Transfer of Ownership of Cultural Property, and for recent treatments of the field, "Loot, legitimacy, and ownership: The ethical crisis in archaeology" (Renfrew, 2000), and "Looting and the world's archaeological heritage: the inadequate response," *Annual Review of Anthropology* 34, 343-61 (Brodie and Renfrew, 2005). But we pass lightly over such avoidable failings, because—to be honest—real archaeological projects probably make more for sitcom or soap opera than for high drama.

11 The art design for some of the underground charnel houses leaves me wondering at the gory logistics. How much murderous killing can one population support?

kid with adrenaline sports skills into a badass survivor with a decent degree of emotional realism. Lara-you starts with *nothing*; stranded, wounded, alone, in pain. As you progress, Lara-you levels up in badassery without ever leaving the acknowledgment of *this is going to hurt* entirely behind. On an emotional level, this works, I feel, supremely well: it's the first time that a "zero-to-hero" narrative has actually *worked* for me. And it's the first time that I remember seeing a game address consequences for engaging in one's first act of serious interpersonal violence, a visceral reaction of shock.

It's also the first time I've seen female friendship drive the narrative arc of a videogame. Aside from surviving and regrouping with other survivors, Lara-you is driven to try to rescue her best friend Samantha Nishimura from the hands of the leader of the weird cultists who live on the island—cultists who seem to think Sam and a sacrifice are the key to controlling the storms that keep all the wreck survivors stranded in place. (I'm still gleeful with unholy delight that it *centers female friendship*! Not just features, but *centers!*)

There are several characters besides Lara, and they're all well-drawn examples of human beings. Not to mention surprisingly diverse for a videogame. High drama, snark, and sacrifice dog everyone's footsteps: you rapidly get a sense for them all as people, and care about what happens to them.

Some of the art is gorgeous. Gameplay, at least on the Xbox, is intuitive and tends not to get in its own way. I've played through twice now (on Easy: story interests me far more than testing my twitch-reflexes) and while death dogged my footsteps, the game's autosave feature is damn handy: it saves *everywhere*. Puzzles tend to be fairly straightforward. It's a game that comes together easily and really *works*.

And yes, I really bloody loved playing a game that owes much to FPS mechanics and has a female character in the central role; a game with an immensely compelling narrative approach and solid characterization; a game that centers female friendship and *doesn't* give us an obligatory male love interest.

I want more games like this. More like this, dammit. Bad archaeology (*cough*LOOTERS*cough*) and all: I felt so god-damn *happy* and *welcome* and *at home* playing *Tomb Raider*, it only reinforced how often before I've felt alienated by a game (or by a film, but that's another story).

Is this how guys feel most of the time? Because the difference is shocking.

Thinking About *Dishonored*

Sleeps With Monsters: Tor.com, March 19, 2013

Let's digress, today, and talk about a videogame.

Okay, so it's not much of a digression for some of you lot. But me, I play maybe two or three games per annum. Four, in a bumper year. Five—if something wild and strange has happened, maybe.

At the time of writing, I've spent much of the past four days sleeping and playing *Dishonored*. And I want to look at it in a limited way from a feminist viewpoint: not necessarily a theoretically advanced viewpoint, but my own experience of playing it.

You are Corvo Attano, the once-trusted bodyguard of the Empress. Framed for her murder and empowered with supernatural abilities, you become an assassin to seek revenge on those who ruined your life. The choices you make will shape your fate and that of the empire around you.

That's what the box copy says. Ever since I played *Metal Gear Solid* for the old Playstation, I've had a terrible fondness for stealth games. Murder! In the dark! Outwitting the enemy *in secret*! But I like RPGs much better, and as a consequence in the last five years—with the exception of last year's *X-COM: Enemy Unknown* and a couple of the SOCOM games—you can pretty much imagine what I've played. The *Mass Effect* series. *Dragon Age: Origins* and *Dragon Age 2*. *The Elder Scrolls: Oblivion* and *Skyrim*.

And I guess they've spoiled me, in terms of being narratively acknowledged. To me, *Dishonored* is more an interesting failure, one whose failings annoy me more the more I think on them.

Before I unpack what I mean by that, let me tell you what *Dishonored* did right by me. The worldbuilding, in terms of mood and detail, is rich and atmospheric: the city of Dunwall, where the game is set, is a port city in the grip of a devastating plague. Graffiti, rats, dead bodies and decay, battered buildings, gaslamp-style science-magic, a fascistically omnipresent security apparatus, and a shocking amount of corruption. The mechanics of creeping around and disposing of your enemies by stealth are well done and mostly intuitive, and you can collect supernatural powers—like teleportation, stopping time, and possessing other creatures—following your first encounter with the slightly creepy being known as the Outsider.

Narratively, it's fairly predictable. Some of the decisions made by the greater narrative were obvious from very early on. One Big Twist—that your allies are using you for their own ends and will end up betraying you—is fairly obvious from the get-go to anyone who's ever read a spy thriller. But there's no way to get the drop on those allies, even if you see the betrayal coming. Choices in-game are limited largely to performing the missions with minimum chaos or maximum bloodshed. This affects end-game results. (Save the child-empress and the city/cause everything to go to hell in a handbasket: these are the opposing poles of the outcomes.)

As failings go, that's a fairly minor one. No game can be all things to all people, and that I wanted the narrative lability of an RPG when that's not *Dishonored*'s goal in life is on me. But its alienating choices with regard to gender and race? Those are on *it*.

Let's start with the first thing that irritated me in its thoughtlessness. The thing is, in *Dishonored,* you never see your own character's face. Corvo never appears on-screen, except in a couple of still-shot endgame frames. So what's the reason to gender that character? You could write all the incidental dialogue without gendered pronouns—it might not be trivially easy to make it sound entirely natural, but it's certainly within the realm of the practical.

The second thing I noticed: Dunwall, although explicitly characterized as a port city and the heart of an empire, is populated only by the whitest of white people. Do I have to point out why this is alienating and wrong, or can we all agree that port cities, even plague-ridden ones, can be expected to present a wider palette of humanity?

Which brings us to item the third: presenting and portraying female characters. Women appear in *Dishonored* in the following roles:

- servants
- one dead empress
- one prepubescent child heir
- one witch, alignment (apparently) chaotic evil
- a handful of harmless survivors hiding in sewers
- aimless corrupt nobility at a masked ball
- the Lord Regent's lover, described to your character in terms of her arse and not her political importance.

Men can be admirals, scientists, thugs and gangleaders, noblemen scheming for advantage, religious leaders, assassin-chiefs, random useful NPCs—the decisions of men *move the game's narrative arc*. Women are pieces on the board.

Is it really so much to ask, in a game set explicitly in a port city, that the characters not be ALL SO WHITE? That some of the chief schemers and powerful movers-and-shakers be not ALL SO MALE?

I complained about this to Twitter. As a result, I was pointed at an article from The Mary Sue.[12] In it, writer Becky Chambers advances the thesis that *Dishonored* made an active, fully thought-out choice in depicting a society with retrogressive gender roles.

The fact that the game points out inequality shows that it's not complicit in it. It wants you to think about it. It wants you to know that such things aren't right.

12 http://www.themarysue.com/but-alas-she-is-a-woman-how-dishonored-uses-gender-roles-to-tell-a-story/.

Unfortunately for my willingness to agree with Chambers' point, *Dishonored* is fairly subtle in how it points out the un-fairness/misery/unpleasantness of discriminatory gender roles. In fact, if you weren't *already* thinking about gender roles, you might not even notice the subtle points—

At one stage in my playthrough, I came across one of Corvo's allies peering through a keyhole, while on the other side a woman was taking a bath. It did not occur to me until later—much later, in fact—that Corvo could've peered through that keyhole too, since looking through keyholes is a key part of all the sneaking. Had I chosen to look, would I have been *rewarded* with a view of an unaware woman who had not consented to be looked on in her nakedness? I don't know—I don't *want* to know—and thinking about the possibility makes my stomach turn over with disgust. The mere fact that one of Corvo's allies is a peeping Tom and the game would not let me kill him at that point in time....

Elizabeth Bear wrote recently:

> I do not actually think those jokes were intended to hurt me. I think they were intended to be funny.
>
> And yet, they left me feeling like a bad person. They left me lying awake at night, wondering why people hated me because I happen to be female.
>
> ...And they don't realize that they are alienating me. A human being. Somebody who will lie awake at night wondering why they hate her.[13]

That? That sentiment describes how I feel about that moment in the game. It makes me want to say to Chambers' defense of the game's choices with: *I respect your point of view. But.*

Gender-based discrimination is unfair, and unethical, and wrong. (And any argument about the game's choices with regard to gender leave out its choices on race.) But. I don't need the social disabilities of my gender slapped in my face in a gaslamp

13 http://matociquala.livejournal.com/2173589.html.

fantasy stealth-assassination game. I don't want to be thinking about how my options were limited *from my birth* by social constructions of gender: how I can look at a slate of political candidates and find so few women, look at a list of members of a corporate board and find so very few women; look at the upper echelons of the civil service and see that women are still outnumbered there.

And if you do shove a society where gender-based discrimination is the norm in front of me in the name of entertainment, then I bloody well want more *range*: noblewomen scheming to control their children's fortunes, courtesans getting in and out of the trade, struggling merchants' widows on the edge of collapse and still getting by; more *women-as-active-participants*, less women-as-passive-sufferers. I would say this sort of thing annoys me, but really that's the wrong word: it both infuriates and wearies me at the same time. I'm tired of needing to be angry.

It's a massive failure at the heart of a game that's smart about all kinds of things—but only as long as white men are the whole of the foreground. Only that long, and no longer.

Part 6.
In Which I Am Wrong on the Internet:
Views and Shorter Pieces

Discussions of Canons, Queer Female Narratives, Older Women in SF, Fantasy Films, Endurance and Persuasion, Cop-out Arguments, Divine Possibilities, and the Clash of Expectations

How Bren Cameron Is Like a Regency Heroine: On C.J. Cherryh's Foreigner books

Essay: First appearance

I came to *Foreigner* (1994) late, with mixed expectations. I have a history of bouncing off C.J. Cherryh's work: *Downbelow Station* (1981), *Fortress in the Eye of Time* (1995), *The Paladin* (1988)... others whose names I don't now recall. And yet more and more people were recommending *Foreigner* and its sequels to me. Ann Leckie, whose *Imperial Radch* books occupy a place very near my heart, claims the Foreigner series as one of her major influences. What felt like dozens of friends would react with startlement when I mentioned I hadn't ever read more than a few chapters of anything by Cherryh—"You haven't read *Foreigner*?! But *why not*? I really think you'd enjoy it!"

It turns out that they were right, and I was very wrong to have resisted reading *Foreigner* for so many years. (In my defense, I think I first *heard* of it only eight years ago: as I write this, it's thirteen years older than that, so I haven't been ignoring it as long as I might have been!) *Foreigner* is, indeed, a novel I found immensely enjoyable—as are those five of its sequels that I've inhaled up to the time of this writing. But it's enjoyable in a way that's made me think more closely about what makes an interesting protagonist and what kinds of stories make for interesting science fiction—because Bren is an unusual protagonist, at the center of an unusual narrative, and I really find it fascinating as an example of the kinds of stories that science fiction *can* tell, but rarely does.

Bren is *Foreigner's* main character. He's a diplomat: the only human diplomat to the alien atevi. Humans started (and lost) a war with the steam-age atevi several hundred years ago, when they first landed on the planet from their dying space station, abandoned by their spaceship. The atevi don't think in human patterns: they do not have love, or friendship, but think in terms of associations. Bren is the only interface between humans and atevi, tasked with releasing human technology to the atevi in a slow, controlled fashion: guiding it so that it does not disrupt atevi society, and preventing another war.

Bren's surrounded by atevi. His role as diplomat—interpreter, sole human-atevi interface—isolates him from other humans, but as a human he's always set apart from the atevi around him, too. His isolation is a strong component of his characterization: the relationships he forges with atevi are not and can never be the same as human relationships, but in a way it seems his loneliness drives him to identify more and more with the atevi and atevi society—different as it is from what is normal and instinctive to humans.

Atevi are larger than Bren is and stronger than he is, and what power he has among them is borrowed, negotiated, traded out of manners and leverage and infinite courtesy. His is soft power, exercised in domestic contexts as much as in public: over the breakfast table, at dinner, over tea and quiet meetings as much as in formal convocations. And although he does—far more frequently than any diplomat reasonably should—often find himself in situations where he's at risk of violence due to the atevi's habit of…robust…political maneuvering, he tends to let his bodyguards do the hard work of keeping him alive. He's not an action hero: he sometimes thinks of himself as a maker of dictionaries. He's seldom the person in charge: more often, he's the person who has to persuade the people in charge to co-operate or to act in ways that won't come back to bite them in the arse later. He's frequently cast headlong into rapidly developing situations with insufficient information and insufficient support, and has to negotiate them on the fly—and arrive at a solution that makes everyone happy. Or at least, less unhappy.

There are remarkably few SFF novels centered on non-action-hero diplomats, on people whose careers—and lives, at times—rely on talking their way out of trouble. There are fewer writers who can make meetings riveting and imbue the tea service with political tension and dark undercurrents. Cherryh mostly succeeds in creating this tension, in giving emotional payoff from the possibility of political and personal upheaval over the dinner table, in making the reader sympathize with alien perspectives, and in making Bren's continuing uncertainty about his own competence—he's extremely competent! he's just constantly working right on the very edge of his competence!—both believable and a source of ongoing tension.

Peculiarly, in many ways Bren rather reminds me of a Regency romance heroine—not for any romantic escapades, but for the tools with which he navigates his world. Fashionable clothes. Servants who manage his household. Perfect etiquette, while knowing how to apologize for breaking etiquette into pieces and doing something new. Having a good relationship with the powerful elderly grandmother of the top local aristocrat. Enduring reversals. Persuading people to see things his way with charm and logic rather than force or wealth.

Bren's strength isn't defined by his physical presence or his ability to bring force to bear on a problem—among the atevi, he's small and puny. Instead, the core of his strength is his intelligent empathy: his ability to understand, at least intellectually, alien perspectives. To engage in dialogue with people who are very different than he is, never seeing them as anything other than people, even though they aren't human. The *Foreigner* books valorize not violence, as so much popular science fiction does, but dialogue and negotiation. It's an approach I'd love to see more of.

The Canons of Proportionality;
Or, on Learning about Literary Canons

Essay: First appearance

I had no idea that literary canons were a thing until, I think, sometime after I started in university. Maybe I knew before then, in a vague sort of way, that there were books you were *supposed* to have read; books that "everyone" had read, for certain values of *everyone*; books that were referenced in almost every discussion of literature or narrative. Particularly in English class in my secondary school, where a general assumption existed that everyone had read *Pride and Prejudice* and some part of Dickens, even if they were never set course texts. (I resisted the entire concept of assigned reading in school with a disdain only possible for the kind of young person who already read widely for pleasure. What do you *mean*, I have to answer *exam questions* on this thing we're reading to death? *There is no joy in this!*) But it wasn't until I hit university and, roughly around the same time, wider contact with Internet communities[1] that I twigged to the concept of canon.

I should note, mind you, that I come to the study of literature as an amateur, in the fullest sense of the word. My educational background is in ancient history, though my interests have occasionally led me sideways into anthropology and religions and the history of more modern times. My exposure to the idea of *literary canon* comes primarily from its defenders, who appear to frequently be the same people who believe that the world has gone downhill since the Elder Days, when young people respected their elders and the quality of education was higher.

The idea of literary canon baffles me, to be honest. The idea that there could ever be a *defining* set of texts, established either

1 Late adopter. Yep.

as the hallmark of quality or the paradigm of (a certain sort of) literature? It's ridiculous. Fortunately, it looks to have largely fallen out of fashion this century, except as a stick in the culture wars.

It's a peculiar stick, though. A peculiar mirage. One that remains in some way attractive: the idea that there are *bounds* within which one can be, perhaps, an expert; perhaps an insider; perhaps a cut above the outsiders. It's closely connected to the idea of good and bad taste, which Pierre Bourdieu critiques in *Distinction* from an anthropological point of view. The very idea of canon is related to cultural capital, to the social and cultural reproduction of class- and status-based social groups. From an anthropological perspective, the whole idea of literary canons is *fascinating.*

Because even when you're arguing over a canon, or multiple canons, you're arguing over a social construct. An illusion that is revealed as such upon close examination. And nowhere is this more obvious than in science fiction and fantasy. The literature of ideas (the literature of, to borrow a phrase, testing to destruction[2]), the literature that sometimes considers itself—in science fiction's case, at least—to be a literature concerned with the possibility of the future, is a literature that positively delights in arguing edge cases, definitions, and the whole concept of a canon.

But, from a social perspective, within SFF fandom the idea of a canon retains a certain currency, in the form of the idea that one should have *done the reading* in order to participate in discussions of science fiction and fantasy. One cannot, for example, discuss fantasy without holding J.R.R. Tolkien in mind, and these days, George R.R. Martin's popularity has made him impossible to overlook. Maybe this is as much an issue with fandom as a social group (or set of overlapping social groups) as it is with the idea of literary canon: perhaps if the idea of literary canons had never been invented, there would be other ways of drawing distinctions between who's *in* and who's *out.*

2   I believe I owe Elizabeth Bear for that one.

But the idea of literary canons does exist, and it is frequently used as a gatekeeping tactic. Have you done the reading? Have you read the right things? Are you really one of us, or are you a Fake Geek (Girl)?

I haven't done the reading. Not all of it. Everything I know about Arthur C. Clarke and Andre Norton, Jack Vance and Isaac Asimov is second-hand; I still haven't read *The Left Hand of Darkness* (1969), and I don't think I can say anything useful about either Samuel R. Delany's work or George R.R. Martin's when I've only read two each of their novels. And while I have vague memories of reading *Stranger in a Strange Land* (1961) and *Friday* (1982), time has blurred my fuzzy recall to an impressionistic palette of *WTF?* regarding Robert E. Heinlein's work rather than anything more…lasting.

Maybe, then, I'm a Fake Geek. But I think this kind of gate-keeping is, finally, at long last, on its way out. Out of necessity, if nothing else.

Arguing about science fiction and fantasy with reference to a historical perspective is something you'd think I'd be more sympathetic to than I am: my academic background is, I might have mentioned, in ancient history. But I think the urge, *today*, to hold up bits and pieces of SFFnal literature as somehow more canonical, somehow more *definitional*, than others is fairly pernicious. The number of novels that fall within SFF's broad and fuzzy boundaries—to say nothing of films, videogames, short stories, television shows—published in any given year is completely out of proportion with what any one person can read. And this has been true for decades now. Any attempt to construct a canon for the purposes of gatekeeping is, of necessity, reductionist. And likely to not only leave out much more than it includes, but also to reflect the biases of those who try to construct it—and thus reinforce existing prejudices.

Besides. Canons. That's not how we come to books, as readers—not unless we're reading to a syllabus. And it's not how books become part of our own interior definitional landscape, our own *particular* literary establishments. The books that shape our views of literature and of the literature of the fantastic are different for each of us. The texts that shaped *my* understanding of what science fiction and fantasy is, and what it does, are intimately peculiar to me.

There are two sets of works, which I came across at roughly the same time in my adolescence, that split my *ideas* of the fantasy and science fictional landscape wide open. Until I was seventeen or eighteen, with some notable exceptions, my reading—my personal canon—had been dominated by epic fantasy in the mold of Robert Jordan, Janny Wurts, and Terry Goodkind;[3] and space opera in the mold of Timothy Zahn's *Star Wars* tie-ins and David Weber. I read what was available in bookshops and libraries, and what I knew to look for—and I looked for these writers because at least they put *women doing things* in their novels.

There were a disproportionate number of books available *without* women doing things. *Plus ça change, plus ça même chose.*

But then—*then*—I ran into the novels of Jacqueline Carey and Lois McMaster Bujold. *Kushiel's Dart* (2001) and *Shards of Honor* (1986)—and all the other Barrayar novels through *Komarr*, let's be honest—and they redefined my mental landscape of what sorts of science fiction and fantasy stories were even *possible*. (I also rather suspect they have, each in their own ways, strongly influenced the wider field.)

But my personal canon is wide and ever-growing, not static—much like literature itself. The idea of a single ideal canon, an *objective* canon, is only possible if one imagines there is only one way of seeing and relating to the field. There isn't. We all come to it via different paths and from different angles.

Canon has to be plural and subjective, or it's just another tool for shutting people out. That? That makes it a really ineffective stick in any sort of gatekeeping exercise. There are always more

3 One of these things is not like the others.

people outside the gates. Just like there are always more books outside *any* sort of literary canon.

Queer Female Narratives in Science Fiction and Fantasy

Essay: First appearance

I didn't expect this piece to require quite as much personal reflection as it seems to need. The first draft pretended to something like objectivity—and it was as stultifying a mess of writing as I've ever produced. In the interests of *not* boring all concerned, I'm just going to embrace the personal narrative—this isn't about queer female narratives in a couple of books. Let's be honest: it's about queer female narratives *and me*.

Much ink is spilled, much breath spent, about the importance of representation. The politics of representation, even. Turns out the political is more personal than I knew: it wasn't until I started seeing queer women in fiction, having non-heterosexual relationships, that I realized I could be—that I *was*—something other than heterosexual myself. Shouldn't really be a revelation to a person in their mid-to-late twenties, should it? And yet, for a very long time I could not even articulate *that* I had sexual or romantic desire, much less sexual desire that operated outside primarily heterosexual modes.

I thought my sexuality *was* celibacy—and I'm still figuring out what it means for me that it might not have to be.

Some of us are a bit...dim? A bit slow to realize what is possible? A bit sheltered, maybe. Without a *positive* portrayal of possibilities other than those by which we grew up surrounded—without those possibilities being rendered obvious and central, acceptable and acknowledged—some of us will only realize late, if at all, that those possibilities are open to us.

What I'm saying is, encountering positive portrayals of queer women having healthy, happy relationships proved revolutionary to me. And remains so: it continues to be a shocking jolt of validation. Portrayal is, in a sense, permission. Permission to be.

Permission to hope for happy endings. (As I write this, Ireland is convulsing with the campaigns for the May 2015 Marriage Referendum, to amend the Constitution so that "Marriage may be contracted in accordance with law by two persons without distinction as to their sex," and permission to hope for happy endings has never seemed more important.[4])

So often, though, narratives have not treated—and still don't treat—queer womanhood as equally valid or equally normal. Too often, when it's brought into focus, it's shown as something either titillating or tragic. Titillating and predatory, even: the woman who preys on other women, whose portrayal is bound up with social discomfort around active female sexuality. Or whose relationships exist for the gratification (sometimes the education, but often the gratification) of a presumed straight male consumer. Or tragic—in a context that denies the validity of their feelings or existence, and sees their relationships either nonexistent or doomed.

It makes an interesting contrast to look at Elizabeth Bear's *Karen Memory* (Tor, 2015) and Seth Dickinson's *The Traitor Baru Cormorant* (Tor, 2015; published in the UK as *The Traitor*) side by side. *Karen Memory* is a steampunk action-adventure novel set in a Seattle-like 19th century American city, and a novel from a writer a decade into her career; *The Traitor Baru Cormorant* is a debut novel, a fantasy in the epic mode, set in various regions under the control of a eugenicist empire with bureaucratically dystopian degrees of social control. One has for its protagonist— the eponymous Karen—a youthful prostitute in an upper-class bordello; the other's main character, the titular Baru Cormorant, is the child of a colonized nation who grows up to become an

4   On Saturday, 23 May 2015—a fair and sunny day—we learned that the Irish people had approved the 34th Amendment to the Constitution by a majority of 62%, with an electoral turnout of over 60%. Following the commencement of the Marriage Act 2015 on 16 November 2015, which gave legislative effect to the statute, marriage equality is the law of the land in the Republic of Ireland.

accountant, highly placed within the imperial hierarchy. One is a very well-written book that I loved all the way through; the other is technically well-written work where I stopped halfway, skipped to the end, and finished by wanting to punch the author. (Sorry, Seth.)

Both protagonists are queer women operating in contexts where a sexual or romantic relationship with another woman is to greater or lesser degree either condemned or not recognized as valid by the respectable strata of their societies. Both the degree to which each of these narratives constructs the social disapprobation of homo-erotic relationships and the degree to which said disapprobation is emphasized within the text are very different.

Karen Memory supports the idea that queer relationships can end happily, despite strife and pain; *The Traitor Baru Cormorant* is grand high tragedy.

Not that I have anything against tragedy. Tragedy's classic, a vital part of the human experience, a necessary part of the story-telling repertoire. But in *The Traitor Baru Cormorant*'s case, the tragic climax to the protagonist's queer relationship repelled me—viscerally, physically. Not because it is itself tragedy, and falling into a long tradition of narratives involving queer people whose relationships are doomed from the outset: no, not that. Or not that alone.

You see, the world in which *The Traitor Baru Cormorant* is set is dominated by an empire that criminalizes sexual "deviance"—tribadism, sodomy, sexual intimacy between people of the same gender—and applies "corrective" measures that range from medicalized operant conditioning (including what may most appropriately be termed rape) to mutilation. Baru Cormorant's birth culture was much less repressive along these lines, but she has (of choice and necessity) worked to assimilate herself into the empire's hierarchy. She is aware of herself as a woman who desires other women, and aware, too, that this desire places her in no small degree of peril, should it be publicly revealed. But she has no community of people who feel likewise. Indeed, there is barely a suggestion that such a community might exist under the empire's apparently stringent social monitoring. One cannot escape the knowledge that the writer made a conscious choice to construct a setting in which queer desire is cast as beyond the social pale, and to shape a queer relationship within that setting that culminates in tragedy: the combination is a kick in the teeth, a jarring reminder of otherness. One made all the more jarring for how rarely one comes across a mainstream fantasy in the epic mode novel with a queer female protagonist. It's *very rarely*—as if you didn't already know.

Contrast that with *Karen Memory*'s approach. The main characters of *Karen Memory* are all people who occupy, essentially, subaltern roles within their society. Karen and her co-workers have a profession that already puts them beyond social approbation: prostitutes have never been a well-protected class. The woman with whom Karen falls in love is further down the scale of respectability: Priya comes from India and was trafficked into sex work at a far less reputable venue than Karen's bordello. But Karen's coworkers—a variety of women, whose own sexual preferences never make it onto the page[5]—form a community who support each other. Already beyond the pale of society's approval, they protect each other, too. Within that community, Karen and Priya's relationship receives no disapprobation. And *Karen Memory* ends on a positive note for that relationship: the opposite of tragedy.

There are still few enough representations of queer women as protagonists in fantasy novels. Few enough that each carries disproportionate weight. Few enough that each gives rise to very *personal* reactions in me. Because portrayal is still, to me, permission—and portrayals that end in tragedy, with no possibility of queer happiness, feel like having part of my own future denied. That's why I'll sing *Karen Memory*'s praises all day, and why *The Traitor Baru Cormorant*, for all its technical successes as a

---

5   For all that *Karen Memory* stars sex workers and takes place in or around brothels, it is a novel that resolutely refuses to titillate.

long-form work of prose, makes me want to hit something. It's not rational. Then again, it doesn't have to be.

Where Are the Older Women?

Sleeps With Monsters: Tor.com, January 29, 2013

When you lay out the recent examples of older women in science fiction and fantasy, you find a decided lack.

Or at least I do. Let me explain.

By "older," I mean women whose concerns are those of motherhood, middle age, *old* age: women who believe in their own mortality, who wear the weight of their pasts as well as their responsibilities to the future, who have a place in the world: a place that may or may not be comfortable, or suitable, but worn in around the edges and *theirs*. By *in science fiction and fantasy* I mean acting as protagonists, or as mentors whose importance to the narrative is not sidelined or minimized by relentless focus on the youthful angst of less mature characters.

I came up with a list. Lois McMaster Bujold leaps right to its head. Ista dy Chalion is the protagonist of *Paladin of Souls*, a book that had a profound effect on me when first I read it, and continues to affect me deeply even during rereads. A woman of forty, whose children are either dead or grown, whose husband died long ago, whose mother has only recently passed away, she has spent most of her adult life suffering the effects of a curse that led to her madness, and to her being thought mad and delicate still. Even though the curse was broken.

The way in which the curse acted upon Ista is painfully familiar. Her grief may have been strange and at times extravagant, but she could see a danger to which others were blind, and her family and society's refusal to believe her is strongly reminiscent of the operation of gaslighting. If the term "gaslighting" is unfamiliar, see Wikipedia for a brief overview.

She's a woman striving to move out beyond the roles others have appointed for her—or that long use has accustomed her to, herself—to discover who she is when she has the choice to act for herself on her own account. It is a profoundly hopeful book, even in its darkest moments, for this narrative of agency not *rediscovered*, but *reclaimed*.

Bujold also gave us Cordelia Naismith, of course: a women mature in her life and advanced in her career, whose "shopping!" scene in *Barrayar* is iconic in its maximum deployment of Awesome in the minimum amount of space.

> Count Piotr's hand slapped down hard on the table. "Good God, woman, where have you been?" he cried furiously.
>
> A morbid lunacy overtook her. She smiled fiercely at him, and held up the bag. "Shopping."
>
> For a second, the old man nearly believed her, conflicting expressions whiplashed over his face, astonished, disbelief, then anger as it penetrated he was being mocked.
>
> "Want to see what I bought?" Cordelia continued, still floating. She yanked the bag's top open, and rolled Vordarian's head out across the table. Fortunately, it had ceased leaking some hours back. It stopped face up before him, lips grinning, drying eyes staring. (Bujold, 1991, 353)

After Bujold, the next writer to use women of maturity as protagonists who comes to mind is Sir Terry Pratchett. Pratchett has his flaws, but the elderly buddy-act of Granny Weatherwax and Nanny Ogg steal every scene they're in from the very moment of their first appearance together, in *Wyrd Sisters* (1988). Granny and Nanny are caricatures of particular sorts of elderly women, of course—the woman who never married and is *quite* happy that way, *thank you*, mind your own business *if* you please, who aged into terrifying sternness; and the terrifyingly friendly old lady with what seems like millions of grandchildren, all of which she is prepared to talk about at the drop of a hat while giving advice on the best way to catch a man and make babies of your own, *cackle cackle rude joke*—but Pratchett's particular genius is to take caricature and make character *anyway*. They're heroic, in their own commonsense, no-nonsense, manipulative *for your own good*, proud, prickly, and interfering ways, sticking an oar in to get rid of annoyingly bad rulers, evil relatives, wicked elves, modern vampires, and so on. And to thwart opera ghosts.

And it's always struck me as unbearably funny, and also apt, that the dwarf name for Granny Weatherwax is "Go Around the Other Side of the Mountain!"

The third writer who comes to mind, mostly because I just finished a reread of her *New Amsterdam* collection, is Elizabeth Bear. A number of the New Amsterdam stories feature Abigail Irene Garrett, who ages from approximately her forties to very old indeed. Bear's novelette "Bone and Jewel Creatures" (2010), which is set in the same universe (albeit at a different time) as *Range of Ghosts*, also features an old woman at the forefront of events: it positions a *very* old sorcerer and her relationship with her (ex) lover and said ex-lover's son in the central role. *Carnival* (2006), *Undertow* (2007), and the Jenny Casey trilogy all feature women with a significant amount of life behind them.

I'm deliberately excluding immortals and antagonists (especially needlessly wicked ones) from my criteria. Which narrows the list a good bit: apart from these three authors, I can think of very few others writing women of maturity. Perhaps some of Catherine Asaro's characters may count, but Asaro tends to write science fiction with a goodly romance component—and part of my problem with enjoying romance storylines is that they seem to turn otherwise sensible adults into teenagers who forget every lesson about life they ever learned. This does not appear to me congruent with depicting maturity. (Use your words, people. Clear communication is a social good.) I'm certain the forgetting-of-every-lesson happens to some people. But, still. Everyone?

I'd really like if more books featuring older protagonists achieved more recognition. Having to look hard for those books gets frustrating.

Why Are Fantasy Films All About the Men?

Sleeps With Monsters: Tor.com, June 12, 2012

The Avengers. Haywire. The Hunger Games. Snow White and the Huntsman. These four disparate films all have something in common, and it's not just a 2012 release.

With the exception of *The Avengers*, they all cast a woman in the starring role. (In *The Avengers*, the Black Widow may not be the star—but of all the character arcs, hers is the one with the most growth and movement.) Without exception, they all show physically active women.

They all show women who are determined to survive. And, if possible, to triumph.

One of these films is also not like the others. It's not *The Avengers*, with its ensemble cast and massive budget. It's not *The Hunger Games*, based on a novel and racking up more popularity every time you turn around. And it's not *Haywire*, with its comparatively tiny budget and straightforward espionage-thriller action. The film that is *most* unlike the others is *Snow White and the Huntsman*, for the simple reason that *SWatH*—while entertaining—is a terribly incoherent film.

You would think that the people behind *Alice in Wonderland* could have managed less incoherence, given actors as smart and capable as Kristen Stewart and Charlize Theron in the starring roles. Those failings have a lot to do with the filmmakers' laziness and conservatism when it came to employing their star (female) talent—a laziness and conservatism not unique to *SWatH*, but one that makes films like *The Hunger Games* and *Haywire*, not to mention 2011's *Hanna* and 2010's *Winter's Bone*, exceptions in their artistic success.[6]

6 Flawed films can still be artistically successful. Nothing's perfect.

The plot of *Snow White and the Huntsman* goes something like this: Evil Stepmother kills Good King, becomes Evil Queen. Keeps princess (Snow White) a prisoner in the Big Damn Castle. The princess escapes, goes through trials, reaches allies, returns with help, and kills Evil Queen, taking Big Damn Castle back for her own.

We can all agree that this is *SWatH*'s basic arc, right?

There are two major problems with this setup. The first is that the minds behind the production clearly got all their world-building materials in a build-your-own kit, but it was the kind of kit that leaves out the instructions and several crucial frames, joists, and screws. (Everyone's had furniture experiences like that, right?) The second—and to my mind, more important—problem is that they were unwilling to let the character of Snow White actually do the work of being the film's protagonist.

Reflecting on *SWatH*, the yawning tangle in its middle becomes obvious as a structural flaw. Unable or unwilling to tell a coming-of-age story with a martial element focused on a princess, the filmmakers decided to shoehorn two other stories into the mix: the Redemption of a Good Man Hard Done By (the Huntsman looks to be a subset of the martyr without a cause type[7]) and one of the most underwritten love triangles I've ever seen—to the extent that it's not clear there's *supposed* to be a Love Triangle in play until it's much too late for anyone to care.

Instead of permitting Snow White her own trials and her character growth, *SWatH* makes the mistake[8] of putting too much of the emotional emphasis of the film on the Huntsman and the Duke's son William, without changing the structure of the film away from that of the *bildungsroman*. It's not a romance: but the framing of the scenes, the feeling of the beats, suggests that film is engaged with its men on an emotional level that it never quite attains with either its villainess or its putative her-

---

7   See "Martyr Without a Cause" on TV Tropes: http://tvtropes.org/pmwiki/pmwiki.php/Main/MartyrWithoutACause.

8   A structural flaw as well as a failure of feminism.

oine. The film doesn't know what to *do* with Snow White once it gets her out of her prison cell. It's torn between allowing her character some growth and treating her as a prize to be won; torn between empathy for its female characters and a lazy conservatism that prioritizes manpain.[9]

The result is confusion.

While Charlize Theron gives the Evil Queen her best (and her best isn't half bad: she does gloriously mad pretty well), her character is beset by many of the same issues that govern the rest of the film's failures. The Evil Queen is a woman whose entire life has been shaped by her hatred of men (for what they have done to her) and by her compelling need to manipulate and control them by means of her beauty and her magic. Other women are her prey: she only speaks to them when she is taunting them or draining them of life. Other women—in the form of Snow White—are a threat to her power, because they will cause her to lose her beauty and thus her ability to manipulate men.

It is a sympathetic reading to see the Evil Queen's need for beauty as both armor and weapon to defend herself: it would be simpler to see hers as an all-controlling narcissism and desire for revenge, and that reading ties more closely in to her effect on the film's landscape. But there's no escaping the fact that the Evil Queen contends with Snow White not for her own sake but for the sake of a beauty that is tied *explicitly* to controlling male desire and thus men themselves. The Evil Queen is shaped by men and her power (or at least her own conception of her power) depends on the male gaze. She does not exist for herself, but for her reflection in the eyes of others.

A critique of the *soi-disant* "beauty" industry? Perhaps. If so, it's one that falls more than a little short.

Snow White and the Huntsman might be a film that bills the women first, but when you get down to it, it's all about the men. It's this kind of lack of imagination that gives us so few female

9 http://thingswithwings.dreamwidth.org/145564.html.

action-heroes and so few films in which women take top billing. And nearly none of them fantasy.

Endurance and Persuasion—Traits of the Heroine?

Sleeps With Monsters: Tor.com, July 3, 2012

A little while ago, I finished reading Karen Lord's *Redemption in Indigo* (2010). It's a delightful book, with the rhythm of a told story, and draws from a different vein of tradition than our modern doorstopper fantasies. It has the mood of a fairytale. And its heroine, Paama, is unusual among fantasies of all stripes. She is an adult, once-married, famous as a cook, and quietly unflappable.

Not that long ago, either, I wrote about "Mass Effect and the normalization of the Woman Hero" (in Section V above). Commander Shepard's an action hero, and action hero-ing seems to be the most popular style of career for SFF's protagonists. There are other kinds of heroes, and other ways of being heroic, but they emerge more rarely. As Lois McMaster Bujold said in her GOH speech[10] at Denvention in 2008, "[I]f romances are fantasies of love, and mysteries are fantasies of justice, I would now describe much SF as fantasies of political agency."[11] The fantasy of political agency lends itself well to men and women of action: less well to heroines or heroes of a quieter bent.

Young Adult fantasies aside, it's striking that most of the examples I can bring to mind are women: Karen Lord's Paama,

10 Text online at http://www.myspace.com/loismcmasterbujold/blog/423204224.

11 Jo Walton argues *contra* that rather than being the fantasy of political agency, SFF is the fantasy of changing the world. "Rather than your characters needing to have political agency to engage the reader, the world is a character and as such needs to change and your story will be engaged with that change—whatever is happening to the other characters." (See http://www.tor.com/blogs/2008/10/bujoldspeech.) It's a good point, but the fantasies of political agency remain among the more popular of the genre's offerings.

Doctor Who's Donna, Ursula Le Guin's Tehanu, Terry Pratchett's famous pair of witches, Granny Weatherwax and Nanny Ogg. Where their involvement in world-changing events is concerned, their role is as catalyst as much as actor: they bring the quotidian into contact with the numinous. Sometimes, they make the numinous quotidian.

And there are a handful of women who, while directly—even intimately—involved in the development of politics, are never *personally* involved in the kinds of violence in which the action-hero thrives. Ista from Bujold's *Paladin of Souls* is perhaps the best example of this. Forty years old, the mother of a ruler, once mad and still thought to be so, *Paladin of Souls* is her *bildungsroman*, her growth into her own power. Yet it is very much a forty-year-old woman's story, one who has come to self-knowledge through endurance and who has had to live circumscribed. Her triumph is, itself, ultimately a triumph of endurance and self-knowledge: she outmatches her adversary not in strength or power, but in will and trust. It isn't a story one can easily see told with a man in her role: the *kinds* of endurance which Ista calls upon are kinds of endurance which are mostly associated with women's lives.

One may also mention in this connection Jacqueline Carey's Phèdre, from her first Terre d'Ange trilogy. Although intimately connected to politics on several levels as courtesan, exile, and later, noblewoman, her role as a mover of events requires persuasion and endurance much more than violence. She is more a catalyst for violence than its instigator: the violence she initiates personally takes place after all options for persuasion have been exhausted.

If there is a commonality in stories of this kind, it is that women protagonists who are *not* action heroes can be expected to draw on patience and persuasion: their power lies in their ability to endure and to convince. The emphasis is less on overmastering their adversaries (or adversity in general) than on outlasting them. And, if possible, outmaneuvering them.

I can think of two examples from visual media to support this idea. Delenn, the Minbari ambassador on *Babylon 5*, is a builder of consensuses by preference. The early seasons of the show demonstrate both her patience and her persuasive abilities. While the events of Season Three place her in a position where her abilities as a leader are redirected to meet more martial goals, I think it is also a challenge to her endurance—which she overcomes. The violence in which she is involved is rarely a personal or individual struggle: she directs and oversees as much as she engages personally.

The other example is President Roslin from *Battlestar Galactica*. While every character's endurance is challenged by the nature of the threat they face, Roslin's will is further tested by her diagnosis of fatal illness. She does not have the power to compel by force (except inasmuch as those who follow her are willing to use force on her behalf), but must lead by persuasion, and endure the consequences when persuasion fails.

Gentle Reader, what do you think of this sort of story? Or perhaps I should say, this sort of character? Are endurance and persuasion traits that crop up in situations more intimately connected to women? If so, why?

Cop-out Arguments

Sleeps With Monsters: Tor.com, September 25, 2012

As a result of a couple of recent conversations, I've been thinking lately about historical fantasy and the extent to which historical norms may limit a writer's ability to include diverse characters—whether we count diversity in terms of race, gender, orientation, or other (unspecified/name your own).

You will be unsurprised to hear that I consider this argument (these arguments, really, since there are a number of them) a cop-out. Whether it's deployed in the service of fantasy drawing on historical inspiration ("The Middle Ages were just *like that*!"), whether it's used to support the whiteness and straightness of alt-history and steampunk, or whether it comes into play in historical fantasy where the fantastical elements are part of a secret history.

Naming no names of those who've disappointed me, so as not to get bogged down in discussions of niggling details, I want to talk about why the use of these arguments is a cop-out, giving historical examples.

A Rebuttal to the Argument that Women Didn't Do Anything Except Get Married and Die in Childbirth (Historically):

Even if we're only talking high politics, I see you this argument and raise you the women of the Severan dynasty in the Roman empire, Matilda of Flanders, her granddaughter the Empress Matilda, Catherine de'Medici, Marie de'Medici, Queen of France and Navarre, Maria Theresa, Holy Roman Empress, Matilda of Tuscany…I could go on. And I can't bear to leave off mentioning the cross-dressing Hortense Mancini, niece of Cardinal Mazarin, who—after fleeing from her wealthy and abusive husband—ended up presiding over a salon of intellectuals in Restoration London.

I'm less familiar with the Great Women of History outside Europe. But I direct your attention to Raziyya al-Din, Sultan of Delhi for four years; Chand Bibi, Regent of Bijapur and Ahmednagar; Rani Abbakka Chowta of Ullal held off the Portuguese for several decades; the Rani of Jhansi was only in her early twenties when she died fighting in the Indian Rebellion (better known to the British as the Indian Mutiny); Wu Zetian was the only woman to rule China in her own name. Need I say more?

If we're including women who did other things? Whole industries depended upon female labor. The production of clothing, for example. Domestic service. Food production. Crime: look at the records of the Old Bailey Online. Sometimes women went to sea or to war: Mary Lacy, Hannah Snell, and Nadezhda Durova are among those for whom we have testimony in their own words, but a rule of thumb is that where there's one literate, articulate specimen, there are a dozen or a hundred more who never left a record. They wrote socially aware medieval poetry, natural philosophy, travelogue, and theology: they established schools and organized active religious communities in the face of establishment disapproval....

They did, in short, just about everything you can think of.

A Rebuttal to the Argument in Favor of Not Including Lesbians/Transgender/Intersex Characters:

It's a modern invention! They might've been queer, but they kept *quiet* about it! What do you mean, cross-dressing?

Sodomy is far better known than its counterpart. Male-on-male sexual activity has a long recorded history: in ancient Greece it was lionized as the epitome of *eros*, and the Classical world had quite the influence upon western European literature. The history of Sapphic love has been, perforce, rather quieter, apart from Sappho herself: for one thing it wasn't as illegal, and thus doesn't turn up in historical court records with such frequency. But I direct your attention to *Harris's List of Covent Garden Ladies*, an eighteenth-century directory of reasonably successful whores published yearly from the 1760s. There, among the ladies who catered for the male trade, Miss Wilson of Cavendish Square held that "a female bed-fellow can give more real joys than ever she experienced with the male part of the sex," and Anne and Elanor Redshawe advertised their services to "Ladies in the Highest Keeping."[12] And Miss Anne Lister, a respectable woman of the Yorkshire gentry in the first half of the 19th century, left behind her diaries, in which her *amours* with other women are recorded for posterity. Those with much patience are welcome to comb through the records of the Old Bailey Online for women who deceived other women, and married them while pretending to be men: there are more than you might think.

As for historical transgender or intersex persons: well, one's recently been the subject of an interesting biography. James Miranda Barry, Victorian military surgeon, is argued convincingly by Rachel Holmes to have been a probably intersex person, female-assigned at birth, who made a conscious decision to live as a man after puberty.[13] (Barry was the first person to perform a Caesarian section in Africa and one of the very earliest to perform such an operation where mother and child both survived.) His friends, what few he had, seem to have been perfectly aware there was something not wholly masculine about him. After his death, his doctor said he wasn't surprised at the rumor started by the servant who did the laying-out, that Barry was a woman: the doctor himself was of the opinion Barry's testicles had never properly dropped.

I've barely scratched the surface here. I'm tired of watching hackneyed treatments of women in fantasy (Madonna or whore, chaste love interest or sexually insatiable villainess) defended on grounds of historicity. There are more roles for women than are shown as a matter of course. Some of the women who filled these

12 See Rubenhold 2005, *Harris's List of Covent Garden Ladies*; Cruickshank 2010, *The Secret History of Georgian London*; Arnold 2010, *City of Sin*.

13 Holmes, 2007, *The Secret Life of Dr. James Barry*.

roles, historically, were exceptional people. Some of them were ordinary, and their actions only look extraordinary in retrospect because of our *expectations* about what was or wasn't normal.

So, I suppose my *cri de coeur* is this: Dear disappointing authors: disappoint me less. Dear fans of disappointing authors: please find other grounds than historical verisimilitude on which to defend your favorite authors' choices.

Epic Fantasy Is Crushingly Conservative?
Sleeps With Monsters: Tor.com, February 26, 2013

I've been thinking about a question asked by @Gollancz on Twitter. "Epic Fantasy is, by and large, crushingly conservative in its delivery, its politics and its morality. Discuss. And why? (Oh why?)"[14] (7:20 p.m. DST, Feb 20, 2013).

Following, and participating in, some of the conversation that followed—which either took the statement for granted or argued that it was an incomplete characterization of the subgenre—several things occurred to me. The first is that we keep having this conversation, over and over again, without defining our terms. How do we define "epic"? What counts as "conservative"? (It's a word with multiple axes of interpretation.)

Let's start with "conservative." N.K. Jemisin says, "Because the "fantasy" most EF delivers is of white male power & centrality, as much as dragons. That *is* conservativism, now"[15] (@ nkjemisin, 8:00 p.m. DST, Feb 20, 2013). We can agree that conservative, here, is fundamentally concerned with not changing the present default *cultural* narratives of who gets to hold and use power, how, and why. For our genre, for our culture(s) in the US, UK, and Europe, that's white (heterosexual) cisgendered men. Often persons who don't fit these criteria who hold and use power *anyway* are portrayed as wrong, anomalous, wicked. (There are plenty of cultural narratives floating about concerning the moral and occasionally physical degeneracy of non-straight-white-men. Plenty.)

But is epic fantasy really "crushingly conservative"? This, I think, depends on how we define "epic." There's a lack of firm se-

14 https://twitter.com/Gollancz/status/305019274219642880.
15 https://twitter.com/nkjemisin/status/305029337114099712.

mantic boundaries when it comes to distinguishing "epic" fantasy, the fantasy of the world-changing/saving quest, of the knight *sans peur et sans reproche* or its deconstruction, from "sword & sorcery"—which I think we can formulate as the fantasy of *encounter*[16]—and "high" fantasy, the fantasy of politics and kingdoms. If we consider *urban fantasy* as encompassing a wider range than the marketing category of that name, we also have second-world urban fantasy, even *noir*, city-focused fantasy. Lately we have a further modifier in "gritty" or "grimdark"—words which are sometimes used interchangeably and sometimes not.

If *epic fantasy* is second-world fantasy that shapes its arc in the form of a grand mythic quest (or several), that plays with tropes such as the return or re-establishment (or sometimes the purification) of a monarch, then it's, by nature, conservative in structure, and by habit conservative in the political institutions it portrays. But it's not *necessarily* conservative in its attitudes towards power, relationships, and orientation towards divinity. We can find counter-examples, depending on which part of our definition we choose to emphasize—Elizabeth Bear's *Range of Ghosts* is fairly clearly epic, and so is Kate Elliott's work. Alma Alexander's *Changer of Days/The Hidden Queen* (2005) may qualify. Jacqueline Carey's work, particularly her deconstruction of *The Lord of the Rings*. Is N.K. Jemisin's work epic fantasy, or high fantasy, or some combination thereof with other influences? How do we classify Bujold's *Paladin of Souls* or *The Sharing Knife* quartet?

16 To clarify my thought: sword & sorcery isn't defined by the quest, even when quests are taking place during it. For me, it's defined more by its tension between quest/magic as a means of making a living (or as intrusions into regular means of making a living) and its encounters with things numinous, strange, and threatening. This is not the strictest definition in the world, I admit. Petto has a brief discussion of ways of distinguishing sword & sorcery and epic at Everything Is Nice, from 2010, at this URL: http://everythingisnice.wordpress.com/2010/02/20/epic-fantasy-vs-sword-and-sorcery/. (I personally think *The Steel Remains* and its sequel hew much closer to active deconstructions of epic heroes rather than to S&S, but the two veins of traditional fantastical conversation lie very close together there.)

Martin Petto pointed out that there might be more than one thing at work: "a small amount of epic fantasy that deliberately subverts conservativeness of genre but also...a much large[r] chunk that has absorbed epic fantasy as one facet [of all the other fantasy influences on their work]. I think a lot of the supposed counter examples are the latter"[17] (@nine_below, 8:40 p.m. and 8:43 p.m. DST, Feb 20, 2013).

The quintessential epic fantasy, *The Lord of the Rings,* was itself in many ways and for all its many flaws a revolutionary reworking of myth. Patrick Nielsen Hayden points out, "[T]he arc of myth is conservative. That's why it's myth"[18] (@pnh, 2200 DST, Feb 20, 2013).

But I'm caught here, once again, on our lack of semantic certainties. "Epic" in discussions like these frequently means whatever each individual participant wants it to mean: examples that don't meet a participant's own personal criteria are dismissed as insufficiently epic, while other participants may wish to claim them. We're going by feel: what makes George R.R. Martin or Peter Brett or Joe Abercrombie or Sam Sykes (to pick some names that came up on Twitter) *more* epic than Michelle West or Kate Elliott or Sherwood Smith or Scott Lynch? Our vocabulary for discussing the distinctions and permutations of second-world "immersive" fantasy as she is writ has no easy way to discuss gradation.

Discussions and definitions of "epic" fantasy are inherently conservative, it seems to me, but I'm not convinced that epic itself needs to be, or is innately, anything other than structurally conservative. (I'm not going to digress here into epic traditions in premodernity and how we can relate them to genre, though I'd like to: I'm not sure I know enough.) We come back again to a lack of a broad consensus in definitions: *I* like epic, *you* like grimdark, *they* like crap.

17 https://twitter.com/nine_below/status/305039499115769856;
   https://twitter.com/nine_below/status/305040021528928256.

18 https://twitter.com/pnh/status/305059517513756672.

Are we, in fact, looking at a largely post-epic landscape? Is epic a term of art that has lost its *particular* meaning and is now applied as a marketing category that encompasses a much wider range of thematic and structural arcs than the world-saving/changing quest and re-establishment/purification of monarchical institutions? What does that mean for our conversations?

What does that mean for the epic quest?

Urban Fantasy Is Licentiously Liberal?
Sleeps With Monsters: Tor.com, March 5, 2013

In the comments to "Sleeps With Monsters: Epic Fantasy is Crushingly Conservative?" one of the participants suggested that if epic fantasy is held to be conservative (the discussion on what constitutes epic fantasy and whether or not it *is* conservative remains open), perhaps we should discuss whether urban fantasy is "crushingly liberal." For the sake of alliteration, another commenter suggested *licentiously liberal*—so that's what we'll argue today.

Let's start from the same principles as we did last time. How do we define "urban fantasy"? What counts as "liberal"? Liberal, it appears, possesses a straightforward definition, at least according to the dictionary:

a. Not limited to or by established, traditional, orthodox, or authoritarian attitudes, views, or dogmas.

b. Favoring proposals for reform, open to new ideas for progress, and tolerant of the ideas and behavior of others; broad-minded.

But we have more than one way of defining urban fantasy. We may define it as it is presently used as a marketing category—to sketch a brief description, fantasies set in the contemporary or near-contemporary world, usually in large cities, featuring supernatural creatures, frequently told from the point of view of a character engaged either in vigilantism or law enforcement, sometimes both, and often but not necessarily featuring romantic/sexual elements. Into such a category we may fit the work of Laurell K. Hamilton, Jim Butcher's Harry Dresden novels, several books by Tanya Huff, the work of Kim Harrison, of Kelley

Armstrong and Ilona Andrews, and Mike Carey's Felix Castor novels, among many others. We may trace the roots of this sub-genre to the 1980s, to Emma Bull's *War for the Oaks* (1987) and Charles de Lint, and include in it the racecar-driving elves of early 1990s Mercedes Lackey.

But we may in addition define it with particular reference to its *urban* nature, as a fantasy primarily focused on the city, the myths, fears, communities, and alienations of civic life, modern or not. The city, the *idea* of the city, occupies a central locus in human history and thought. Its role is more important than ever in an age where an ever-increasing majority of humans live in cities—by 2030, 92% of people in the UK and over 60% in China, some projections say.[19] I'm inclined to argue that some second-world fantasies, like Max Gladstone's *Three Parts Dead* (2012) or Michelle Sagara's *Chronicles of Elantra* novels or Pratchett's Discworld Ankh-Morpork novels, enter so far into this urban conversation and find the idea of the city so central to their identities that *not* calling them urban fantasy seems a foolish exclusion.

We may suggest a taxonomy—or at least a tag-cloud—of urban fantasy as follows: second-world, historical, contemporary or near-future, investigative, vigilantist, political, soap-operatic, near-horror, romantic, humorous. Within the greater umbrella of "urban fantasy" as I choose to conceive of it, then, it's clear that there are a wide range of possible moods, themes, and approaches. But is it *open to new ideas for progress?*

If we had framed the question: *is urban fantasy progressive in the political sense?* (i.e., does it favor or promote political or social reform through government action, or even revolution, to improve the lot of the majority?), I should have to argue in the main against: popular fiction is seldom *successful* in revolutionary dialectic. Nor, for that matter, has urban fantasy commonly been *culturally* progressive: its gender politics may perhaps improve

19 http://www.guardian.co.uk/news/datablog/2009/aug/18/percentage-population-living-cities.

slightly over those historically typical of fantasy in a pastoralist setting, but true progressivism, particularly in contemporary investigative/vigilantist urban fantasy, is often hamstrung by authors' reliance upon Exceptional Women narratives. As a subgenre, its racial politics are as progressive as the rest of the SFF landscape—which is to say, not very, and prominent popular examples are not common.

Urban fantasy is easier to define than epic fantasy: its semantics are more tightly bounded. But is it easier to assess urban fantasy's relationship with established norms and authoritarianism? Can we actually accurately call it *liberal*, much less "crushingly"—or even licentiously—so?

Divine Possibilities and the Clash of Expectations

Sleeps With Monsters: Tor.com, July 2, 2013

I've recently had the privilege of introducing a good friend to the novels of Lois McMaster Bujold, starting with *The Curse of Chalion* (2001) and proceeding through the Miles Vorkosigan novels.

Discussing books that mean a great deal to you with someone who's reading them for the first time has the odd effect of highlighting both their best points and their greatest flaws: where they work for one person and not another. Ista's journey in *Paladin of Souls* still takes me by the throat and shortens my breath with its power, but its moments of greatest impact—for me—slid off my friend like water, like butter off a hot knife.

The moment where Ista asks the Bastard for her true eyes:

> I have denied my eyes, both inner and outer. I am not
> a child, or virgin, or modest wife, fearing to offend.
> No one owns my eyes now but me. If I have not the
> stomach by now to look upon any sight in the world,
> good or evil, beautiful or vile, when shall I? It is far too
> late for innocence. My only hope is the much more
> painful consolation of wisdom. Which can grow out of
> knowledge alone. Give me my true eyes. I want to see.
> I have to know. (Bujold, 2003, 199 - UK edition)

When Ista encounters the Father on the stair, and passes his blessing to poor doomed Arhys:

> Your father calls you to his court. You need not pack.
> You go garbed in glory as you stand. He waits eagerly
> by his palace doors to welcome you, and has prepared
> a place at the high table, by his side, in the company of
> the great-souled, honored, and best-beloved.
> (Bujold, 2003, 375 - UK edition)

Those passages give me chills, still. And yet, discussing them with others, the depth and power of their impact is far from universal. They seem to hit those of us who are or were once inclined to religious sentiment hardest. I may have been an atheist/agnostic since before I could vote, but I've still had what persons of deistical bent call "religious experiences." One of the most powerful things about Bujold's *Curse of Chalion* and *Paladin of Souls,* one of the things which gives them such emotional weight, is the sense of divinity. *Oh. Oh. That's divinity. That's how it could be.* A sense that calls back cathedrals, roadside shrines, the immense sweep of Delphi.

Numinous is a word sometimes misused. But the Chalion books have betimes been characterized as speculative theology, and it's not a poor description in the least.

But that sense of divine presence only works if you have a background with divine possibility.

Contemporary with watching my friend devour the Vorkosiverse, I've been reading Bujold's latest work myself. *Sidelines: Talks and Essays* (2013) collects Bujold's never prolific nonfiction as an ebook: her speeches; her occasional essays; introductions and afterwords; three travel diaries, from Russia, Croatia, and Finland; a selection of blog posts.

Bujold is never less than interesting. Sometimes thought-provoking, sometimes wise, sometimes frustratingly facile—but never less than interesting. The development of her thought across decades is intriguing to watch, the hazy outline of an intellect whose effects on the SFF pond might not be visible on the surface but who's left profound ripples underneath.

Naturally, this is a work for completists, but it may well appeal to the casual reader who cares to find something brief to dip into to illuminate Bujold's career.

Although *Sidelines* fails to illuminate why the Vorkosigan series reached a pinnacle of emotional impact in *Memory* (1996) and *Komarr* (1998), only thereafter to shy from emotionally challenging its protagonist in any serious way. It is difficult to return to reading space adventure stories in a series where one has seen one's heart wrenched from one's chest and put back in differently: going forward, expectations clash.

Speaking of a clash of expectations: Susan Jane Bigelow's *The Daughter Star* (2013). Its flap copy makes it sound like military science fiction/space adventure, but inside it's a different can of worms entirely, and I'm not sure all the worms are baiting the right hooks. (But the protagonist Marta Grayline is a lesbian; in my view that's at least one point in its favor.)

In many ways—the slow opening, Marta's struggle with her parents and their oppressive mores, her strong connection to her sister—*The Daughter Star* reads like a YA coming-of-age, a discovery of agency and choice. But Marta is in her twenties, and what would be a reasonable reaction to buffeting-by-fate in a younger person reads like passive lack of direction and common sense in an adult.

But there are psychic, mysterious aliens, and a destroyed Earth that may not in fact be dead; secret organizations, war and revolution. Give Bigelow credit for putting much Cool Shit on her skiffy canvas: this would be a good bridge novel between YA and the adult section for people complaining about the lack of non-dystopic YA science fiction.

Afterword

Stories usually have natural endings. This is a collection of opinions, so when it comes to wrapping things up, I have no idea where to even begin. Did you enjoy your guided tour of my reading experience in science fiction and fantasy?

I don't have an argument here. No neat little thesis to tie everything up. Just a handful of observations, and a lot of opinions.

Every so often, one hears the question, "Where are all the women?" Where are all the women writing X, or Y, or Z? (Where are all the women writing SFF criticism?) If you've stuck with this collection thus far—hell, probably if you picked up the collection in the first place—you already know this is usually a question asked from ignorance or from the kind of disingenuous minimizing of women's achievements done by people who aren't interested in an honest answer.

Things are—I do believe—getting better, slowly and by increments. It's a lot harder to ask that question in honest ignorance these days, for one thing. (Though we have a long way to go, and as ever, white women have reaped disproportionate benefit from the progress that has been made.)

If I were a different person, I would end this collection with a call to arms, a call to rise up and be counted. A call for revolution! But the revolution has always been with us. So has the backlash. The surest progress is won by increments and defended—built on—over the course of years and decades. Sometimes, as Seneca wrote two millennia ago, "even to live takes courage" (Seneca the Younger, *Epistulae morales ad Lucilium* 78). In a world where, three decades on from Joanna Russ's *How To Suppress Women's Writing* the same arguments keep being deployed—*She wrote it but*—to minimize the impact and influence, the range and breadth of women's writing, and where the problem of sexual harassment remains a significant issue at conventions (and in life) for female fans and professionals alike, simply speaking up remains a radical act. Simply *remembering* the breadth and influence of the women who came before and the women who are working now is itself revolutionary.

There's a history to remember, and we're all part of it. We are all free to choose our own personal literary canons. Sometimes that means looking for the literary history other people overlook. Sometimes it means making our own history. Sometimes it means living, as best we can.

This collection, I hope, represents one small slice of one single person's engagement with issues surrounding women in the science fiction and fantasy genre literature—mostly literature. It's not a beginning and it's not an ending, and it can never hope to be either definitive or comprehensive. The field is both wide and constantly changing, and no one person can, these days, really gain a truly synoptic view.

I drew the title of the column I have written for Tor.com, "Sleeps With Monsters"—a phrase which, in modified form, provides the title to this collection—from Adrienne Rich's poem, "Snapshots of a Daughter-in-Law" (published in the book of the same title in 1963). "A thinking woman sleeps with monsters/ the beak that grips her, she becomes." In the same section of that poem, Rich writes,

> The argument *ad feminam*, all the old knives
> that have rusted in my back, I drive in yours,
> *ma semblable, ma soeur!*

All we have to do is keep working on getting rid of the knives....

Works Cited

Arnold, Catharine. *City of Sin*. New York: Simon & Schuster, 2010.

Cruickshank, Dan. *The Secret History of Georgian London*. New York: Random House, 2010.

Holmes, Rachel. *The Secret Life of Dr. James Barry*. Gloucestershire, UK: The History Press, 2007.

Larbalestier, Justine. *The Battle of the Sexes in Science Fiction* Middletown, CT: Wesleyan University Press, 2002.

Merrick, Helen. *The Secret Feminist Cabal: A Cultural History of Science Fiction Feminisms*. Seattle, WA: Aqueduct Press, 2009.

Rieder, John. *Colonialism and the Emergence of Science Fiction*. Middletown, CT: Wesleyan University Press, 2008.

Rubenhold, Hallie. *The Covent Garden Ladies: Pimp General Jack and the Extraordinary Story of Harris' List*. Gloucestershire, UK; The History Press, 2005.

Russ, Joanna. *How to Suppress Women's Writing*. University of Texas Press, Austin TX, 1983. British edition, London: The Women's Press Ltd, 1984.

Index

About the Author

Liz Bourke is a cranky queer person who has opinions about science fiction and fantasy a lot. She holds a PhD in Classics from Trinity College Dublin, which means she also has a lot of opinions about history. Her reviews and nonfiction have appeared in *Locus*, *The Cascadia Subduction Zone*, and *Vector*, and online at Tor.com, *Strange Horizons*, and *Ideomancer*.